PR
In A Week

Brian Salter

Also available in ebook

Contents

Introduction   2

Sunday   4
Who needs PR?

Monday   16
External audiences

Tuesday   30
Dealing with the media

Wednesday   44
Social media

Thursday   62
Practical pointers for powerful press releases

Friday   80
Marketing communications

Saturday   94
Internal PR

7 × 7   110

Answers   117

Introduction

'If a boy meets a girl and impresses upon her how wonderful he is... that's Advertising.'

'If, instead, he tells her how lovely she looks, how much she means to him and how much he cares for her... that's Sales Promotion.'

'But if the girl seeks him out because she has heard from others what a splendid fellow he is... that's Public Relations!'

I remember going to a PR conference in the UK once where one of the speakers flashed up this 'definition' of PR on the screen. We all laughed, but, despite our different backgrounds, we could all identify with his theme.

Public relations is the practice of conveying messages to the public with the intention of changing the public's actions by influencing their opinions. By targeting different audiences with different messages to achieve an overall goal, PR practitioners can achieve widespread opinion and behavioural change.

Communications is seen as being a key element in business, with PR experts increasingly called on to advise senior management on appropriate communications strategies, *before* decisions are made, rather than being called on to defend them *after* they have been made.

But PR is not just for self-conscious organizations. If you are looking for a job or an in-house promotion; or if you are trying to publicize a fundraiser for your local charity; if you're trying to advance a cause, or you want others to appreciate your point of view, you need your voice to be heard.

Similarly, politicians of all parties work with PR experts not only to promote their point of view but, at the most basic level, to help them get re-elected!

Even royal families around the world employ PR experts to massage their image for the general public, as do film and pop stars, sports personalities, broadcasters – and, for that matter, anyone in the public eye.

Nowadays there is a veritable plethora of communication channels available, ranging from traditional newspapers and magazines to online outlets including ezines, social networking sites and blogs. Some of these are good in some situations, but hopeless in others.

Throughout this week we will therefore be concentrating on how we can effect the flow of information and how we can achieve the desired mindset change in our target audiences.

Brian Salter

SUNDAY

Who needs PR?

PR – or public relations – is all about getting people to talk about your business in a positive way. Increasingly, companies throughout the world are building links with their various target groups so that they are regarded in a better light by their customers, suppliers and industry regulators.

To a certain degree, PR follows the same principles for small companies as for big organizations – it's just a matter of scale. Even the smallest business can use publicity to broaden its customer base and improve the sales climate for its products.

Significantly, too, many in-house communications departments have matured to a point where they are being asked to drive through significant internal cultural change programmes, in place of – or certainly hand-in-hand with – the human resources or marketing departments.

When it comes down to it, PR is all about communication. It means talking to your stakeholders, whether they are your suppliers, customers... or even your own staff.

Today we will look at the nature of PR, and especially:

- the key role played by communication, including language
- how changing perceptions is the bread-and-butter business of PR
- the importance of the who, what, why and how.

Looking after a company's public image

Public relations is all about human relations – the psychology of interrelating with your different audiences – and a critical aspect of growing any business. Everything you say and do is part of your PR campaign. It is the image you project every day to everyone you meet. It is about you and your company becoming a force in the public eye on a regular basis.

Overall, PR is just one part of the overall marketing mix. It is likely you will also be undertaking other activities such as maintaining a website, getting testimonials and product feedback, sending out newsletters, direct email campaigns, possibly even advertising, and so on.

But, unlike advertising, editorial is usually free and regarded as independent, and therefore more likely to be credible. And many companies have learned that a bit of free editorial is worth many times that amount of space in advertising.

As well as raising awareness of your brand, PR can also be used to educate your target audiences about your position within your particular industry, ultimately (you hope) generating more enquiries and sales leads, as well as traffic to your website and/or shop.

PR can cover a host of activities, such as:

- press releases
- appearances in news stories
- company profiles
- opinion articles
- quotes in features
- product reviews
- case studies
- blog posts
- social media postings
- audio and video clips such as podcasts and video casts
- advertorials
- competitions

PR is not difficult – it's just about common sense (except, as they say, common sense is anything but common!). However, it is time-consuming and you do need to prepare yourself first.

 TIP *PR is, to put it simply, all about communicating your ideas and values to your target audiences.*

Communication

What do we actually mean by communication?

There doesn't appear to be one definition accepted by everybody. It is one of those grand-sounding words which can mean everything and nothing at one and the same time. All businesses need to communicate with their employees if they want the best out of them; with suppliers if they want the right raw materials at the best price; with shareholders if they want to keep them on their side; with customers if they want to make any profit at all, and with the community at large, since no one – let alone any company – can act totally unaffected by those who surround them.

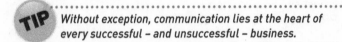

TIP *Without exception, communication lies at the heart of every successful – and unsuccessful – business.*

Successful communication applies as much to manufacturing industries as it does to service sector or public sector organizations. Everyone is involved in one way or another, but the problem is that few people are taught to communicate in a manner that is suitable for business.

In social communication – especially now in this Internet age – we can afford to be sloppy in what we say since, in general, both parties know one another and understand that things left unsaid can be taken as read. However, in a business environment, communication has to be clear, precise and unambiguous and, if you want to avoid misunderstandings at some later date, it needs to be formal in nature and planned carefully.

A two-way process

Communication – whether it involves organizations, individuals or groups of individuals – requires a minimum of two parties. Although one party may be the initial sender of a message and the other the initial receiver, both sides need to take on both roles if successful communication is to occur. This is because feedback – even if only a nod of the head – is essential if the sender is to get confirmation that a transaction has been completed.

Types of communication

The ideas communicated can be **verbal** or **graphical** – verbal encompasses any message that is spoken, written or emailed, for instance, while graphical refers to a message that can be encapsulated as a visual image. (After all, we are always being told that a picture can paint a thousand words!)

Although these **direct channels** are essential elements of communication, there are a number of other **indirect channels** that many businesses ignore, but which can be a major source of poor communication if handled improperly. Think of the importance of body language, for instance. We are all very quick to make instant judgements of people by the way they look or the body signals they give off.

Someone who is unable to keep eye contact and is always looking away from you is likely to be giving off indirect signals that he or she is untrustworthy or certainly not someone you can rely upon, even if the real reason is shyness.

Barriers to communication

Communication can also be prevented or minimized by interference that stops a message from getting through. Extraneous noise, be it someone playing a trumpet in a neighbouring apartment, or someone's ghetto blaster turned up too high, can often divert the receiver's attention from the real message getting through.

However, interference in the form of **preconceptions** on the part of the receiver can also play a major role in a lack of comprehension. If your customers don't trust you as a company because of something they may have heard about you, then it may not matter what you say to them because everything you do say will be treated with cynicism or simply not believed.

Barriers can exist in many different forms, but the effect is the same: core messages are either hindered or stopped altogether from getting through.

The key role of language

Ever since humans set foot on this earth, language has been at the heart of communication. Even babies, who have not yet learned to talk, can still communicate. When they are hungry or unwell or uncomfortable they cry and their carer soon understands that they want feeding or changing, or whatever else they need. It might take the worried parent a while to work out what the problem is, but there is still a communication there, of sorts.

Early humans also expressed their feelings and experiences without using words. Using facial expressions and their hands, they could communicate using body language – something we are still good at today, often subconsciously.

As we developed language skills, people used words to convey what they were feeling. With alphabets, writing gave yet another powerful boost to convey thoughts, ideas and feelings.

Nonetheless, most of us don't have to think very long to come up with names of people we know who are anything but good communicators. There are several reasons for this and some may not always be correctable.

In many parts of the world, most notably in the Middle East and South-east Asia, there is a plethora of foreign expatriate workers who do not communicate using their mother tongue, and of necessity this leads to the use of inappropriate tenses, declensions and conjugations, not to mention the strong regional accents or differences in the use of language on a regional basis. (It is said, for instance, that Mao Zedong could not be understood by many of his audience in Beijing when he declared the new People's Republic of China in front of the Forbidden City, as his Hunan accent was difficult for northern Chinese to understand!)

Yet, despite these apparent drawbacks, it is amazing how well people can communicate with one another even when there is a lack of a common language.

Changing perceptions

PR practitioners work with facts, perception and truth every day. It's what we do for a living. As practitioners, we talk almost casually about changing perceptions – but what does that really mean?

Perception is the process by which humans collect information and a basis for how humans see things. When we talk about changing perceptions, what we actually mean are two things:

1 changing individuals' ways of perceiving
2 changing their understanding and opinions.

This is important to remember because it is easy to ignore one part or the other. PR has two functions – education and persuasion. **Education** seeks to change the way someone perceives an event and **persuasion** seeks to change how the individual interprets facts that have been perceived.

One can have knowledge of a subject and a separate opinion about it that may or may not relate to that knowledge. Knowledge leads to understanding. Opinion is judgement, or a formed conclusion.

There are two basic states of understanding – good or poor. But we can identify *three* possible types of opinion – good, bad or neutral. If the individual is on our side and knows us well, good PR can reinforce his or her understanding and opinion. If the individual knows us well and can't stand us, we try to rebut the person's negative comments about us. If the individual doesn't know us well, but thinks highly of us, we educate that person about us and reinforce the good opinion – and so on.

The who, what, why and how

All organizations need to communicate with a number of **different audiences**, and sometimes what they say to one will not necessarily be the same as what they wish to say to another. Likewise, what feedback they solicit from one may not be what they solicit or receive from another. External audiences, for instance, may be given a slightly glossier picture of the fortunes of a company than those within the organization. There will almost certainly be those, too, who will need to be 'in the know' with regard to any bad news or commercially sensitive information, and so getting to know your audiences has to be a key consideration in any PR campaign.

TIP *There is a very fine dividing line between showing something in a good light and giving misleading information.*

Just as important as identifying the key audiences that you wish to reach and communicate with is knowing what it is you want to communicate and why you are trying to say it in the first place.

If that sounds like simply stating the obvious, then consider how many organizations tend to 'open their mouths before putting their brains into gear'. This week we will be looking at some of the things you may wish to be communicating with your audiences since communications can only really be viewed in a holistic way; otherwise one could argue that the whole exercise has been a waste of time.

Finally, knowing what it is you want to communicate is only half the story. So over the coming week we will also be concentrating on how the flow of information can be effected.

Summary

Today we have seen that the art of public relations is all about the skills of persuasion and of either changing or reinforcing mindsets in order to achieve a particular outcome.

Quite apart from all the other skills needed in carrying out our PR work, the core of good PR comes down to communicating our messages in the most appropriate and accessible ways to our target audiences.

This communication does not just incorporate the verbal messages we give out. The way we behave and conduct ourselves will play a major role in the fortunes of our business.

The way we give out our messages, together with the way we target who are the recipients of these messages, will also play a major role in how well our business performs.

In short, it is no exaggeration to claim that the role that PR plays can be a decisive factor in whether our business is ultimately successful or not!

SUNDAY

MONDAY

TUESDAY

WEDNESDAY

THURSDAY

FRIDAY

SATURDAY

Fact-check (answers at the back)

1. Company communications should be primarily focused on talking to...
   a) Your customers ❑
   b) Your suppliers ❑
   c) Your staff ❑
   d) Anyone who has something to do with your company ❑

2. Internal cultural change programmes should be led by...
   a) The PR department ❑
   b) The HR department ❑
   c) The marketing department ❑
   d) All three together ❑

3. The PR function is primarily to do with...
   a) Maintaining a relationship with the media ❑
   b) Sending out newsletters, press releases and direct mail ❑
   c) Being responsible for the company website ❑
   d) All of the above ❑

4. When comparing coverage of your brand or products...
   a) Editorial coverage is far superior in value to advertising ❑
   b) Editorial coverage carries more credibility than advertising ❑
   c) Editorial coverage offers better value than advertising and is also far more credible ❑
   d) None of the above ❑

5. Which of the following is *not* true?
   a) Communication requires a minimum of two parties ❑
   b) Someone who will not look you in the eye is likely to be untrustworthy ❑
   c) Good communication can be affected by body language ❑
   d) Communication can be verbal or graphical ❑

6. When we talk about changing people's perceptions, what we really mean is...
   a) Changing the way they gather facts ❑
   b) Changing their opinions ❑
   c) Changing their understanding ❑
   d) All of the above ❑

7. In PR terms, it is normally appropriate for external audiences...
   a) To be given only good news about a company ❑
   b) To be told the bad news along with the good to gain credibility ❑
   c) To be given exactly the same information as told to staff ❑
   d) To be given a glossier interpretation of the facts than is given to employees ❑

8. PR is only useful...
a) To large organizations or companies who want to increase market share ❏
b) To small companies who want to broaden their customer base ❏
c) For changing public perception of a company, not of its products ❏
d) None of the above ❏

9. Which of these statements is true?
a) Good communication is not possible between two people who do not have a common language ❏
b) Emailed communications are dangerous because they can be ambiguous ❏
c) SMS should never be used for important communications ❏
d) None of the above ❏

10. If we want to change perceptions, we need to...
a) Change the way people learn about new facts ❏
b) Change people's opinions ❏
c) Educate someone so he/she knows something he/she didn't know before ❏
d) All of the above ❏

SUNDAY
MONDAY
TUESDAY
WEDNESDAY
THURSDAY
FRIDAY
SATURDAY

15

MONDAY

External audiences

We have seen that PR is intimately wrapped up with the way you communicate with your stakeholders: your key publics and your target groups – the people who will receive your communications.

Consider for a moment this list of products and services together with their primary stakeholders:

- hospitals: patients
- stores: customers
- schools: students
- radio: listeners
- airlines: passengers.

In this list, you will see that the target group or public that a hospital has to focus its communications on are its patients. In the same way, stores need to communicate with their customers, schools with their students (and parents!) and so on.

Understanding what drives stakeholders' desires and needs is an important skill in PR, which is all about winning the support of the public by addressing their wants, interests and needs rather than your own. In essence, it is all about psychology.

Today we will be looking at:

- how to promote your company's products and services to the outside world
- how to create a positive image of your company as a whole
- extending PR beyond customers and clients to, for instance, suppliers, financial analysts and government.

First things first

When planning an external PR strategy, your first job is to identify all your audiences before you can even begin to think about what it is you wish to get across to them. Not all of those intended recipients will want the same information, or even require it in the same format. So, to begin with, you need to work out in very simple terms...

● what you are trying to say
● why you want to say it in the first place
● to whom you wish to talk.

How are you going to get your message across?

Many people are so anxious to get talking that they often don't think through what it is that the potential recipient might be interested in finding out! Yet the secret of good communications – and ultimately of PR – is to put yourself in the mindset of your recipients and to think through what it is that you want to say to them that will be of interest to them. That is no easy task.

In addition to the content of your communication, PR is also the result of what you do, as well as what you say, and what others then say about you. For instance, if you were to go for a job interview, the first and most important impression is the one you give on entering the room. Before you even open your mouth to say hello, you will be judged on how you look, your dress, your manner, your attitude and how you speak. Body language is a crucial aspect of the way you will be judged; and a job interview is just as much about successful PR as it is improving the attitude of potential customers or suppliers.

Over the past two or three decades, the way we do business has been turned on its head. Increasing competition – especially from overseas – and a rise in customer expectations means that today's company cannot ignore the need to communicate well with its customers or it will simply fall victim to those competitors – perhaps on the other side of the world – who communicate better. Why, after all, should a prospective customer bother with you if your main competitors are only too happy to communicate with them and you're not?

These communications could be at the simplest level. Think about when you go to the supermarket, for instance. Often there are new products such as shampoos and detergents on display. Perhaps there is also a salesperson describing the advantages of these new products. He or she might even be giving samples of the product to the shoppers or offering a discount.

PR is working here to help launch or introduce new products and encourage people to buy them by:

● creating an awareness about their existence
● differentiating them from similar products in the market.

In a similar manner, companies can remind consumers about existing products, such as a particular brand of coffee or a type of paint, by:

● organizing special events
● putting on displays at exhibitions
● putting together a window display in a shop
● holding media events
● distributing pamphlets and brochures.

So today's organization needs to concentrate on marketing communications as well as on providing customer service and after-care in a way that will retain those customers in the long term. Poor service, a lack of understanding of customer needs and arrogance on the part of the organization are the main reasons that customers become ex-customers, rather than price alone.

A grey area

Of course there is a grey area in which it is difficult to differentiate between 'pure' public relations and marketing communications. But why worry about such distinctions? PR is all about changing and improving attitudes and that means that any communications from a company will have an effect on its reputation, regardless of what you call it.

Measuring opinion

Measuring opinion is a crucial part of building an appropriate or successful PR plan. Not only is communication a two-way process but a company that gets genuine feedback from its customers and target groups will be better equipped to know what messages it needs to put across as well as how to impart them.

Very often companies assume they know what their customers are thinking. However, they tend to see the situation from their own point of view and could be blinded to some of the problems that others experience simply because they come from a different mindset.

For this reason, consumer surveys and questionnaires are widely used to garner the views of prospective customers because they are cheap and easy to organize and can give useful information on demographics of the different marketplaces. The trouble is that they tend not to be very accurate because they usually deal in generalities and they take little account of people's perceptions.

SUNDAY
MONDAY
TUESDAY
WEDNESDAY
THURSDAY
FRIDAY
SATURDAY

In some parts of the world (most notably in Asia), there is a culture of not wishing to offend, and so many people will proffer the answers they feel are 'wanted' by the surveyor rather than say what they genuinely feel.

To a certain degree, the relatively recent introduction of online surveys gets over many of these problems; and better still the results can be near instantaneous as well as much easier to assimilate using data manipulation programs.

Surveys are useful for identifying trends and for getting a 'broad-brush' picture in order to identify areas for more in-depth and specific research, which can then be undertaken in a more specialized and focused way.

Often, the next stage is to set up focus groups which can provide subjective and objective information as well as allow customers to get involved in the decision-making process. Here the composition of the groups is of paramount importance and typically eight to ten participants will be an optimum number. A relaxed environment is essential to encourage open discussion and a facilitator who is experienced in chairing such meetings is necessary to keep the group focused.

The resultant reports and data can prove extremely useful in honing the communication plan and promotional activities, not to mention the possibility of changing the actual product if something major crops up!

Promotional PR

Promoting your goods and services can include a wide variety of activities in gaining the attention of your prospects. Advertising, media relations, events, direct mail, and even the packaging of the goods themselves, say a lot about your company and its products. All play an important part of the communications and marketing mix, building your brand and gaining you market share, as well as letting people know what you as a company stand for.

Promotional activities in the main are all about tempting your prospects by creating a feeling of excitement about your products or services, or a feeling of belonging to a tribe which is associated with your company. There is always a strong temptation when communicating the positives to overplay the benefits that a prospect will get, but exaggeration is something that has a terrible habit of coming back to haunt you at a later date.

The dangers of hype

This is something that advertising professionals must always weigh in the balance. For instance, I remember going to a promotional day in Saudi Arabia for a major 4 × 4 car manufacturer. Hundreds of prospective customers were given the opportunity to test-drive the new model on a desert terrain obstacle course. The banners around the course loudly proclaimed such messages as 'There is no such thing as Cannot!'. How those self-same marketers must have cringed when one of their test cars failed in its attempt to drive up a steep hill and had to be eased down the slope for over ten minutes by an army of helpers pushing and pulling the car in an attempt to keep it on the track.

Customers are becoming ever more discerning because of their greater ability to choose more widely. Most customers only want to get good service and be told the truth about delivery, quality, terms and conditions, and so on. So check all your small print. It may be *legally* right but is it losing you sales because of its attitude?

I'M SORRY. NO KEY FOR YOU 'TILL YOU FILL IN YOUR GRANDMOTHER'S MAIDEN NAME

Case study: poor service = poor PR

A friend of mine recently flew on a major European airline from her home in Beijing to Germany. Unfortunately, she forgot to present her frequent flyer club card at check in and subsequently tried to 'reclaim' her frequent flyer points. Despite being told by ground staff at the German airport that she could do this online, she made three attempts to do so once she had returned to Beijing. She was told that she would have to send in the original boarding passes and purchase receipts to their head office, despite the fact that she was able to quote the eTicket number of the flight, as well as the seat details.

Her response was that, since she could quote the eTicket and flight details to the likes of KLM and Qatar Airways, both of whom could check such details against her current frequent flyer membership, then why couldn't this airline, which is a member of IATA and uses the same ticketing arrangements. The airline, however, was adamant that their rules insisted on them seeing the original ticket stubs. Perhaps this was a hark-back to pre-Internet days; but the result is that my friend swears she will never travel with that airline again.

Multiply that a number of times by others who must have had the same experience and the likelihood is that many people will in future try to fly any other airline rather than this one – simply because of an outdated and illogical 'rule'.

23

Suppliers

The majority of businesses have to get their raw materials from an outside supplier. In the past, traditional communications with suppliers have been on the basis of beating them down to the lowest possible supply price, but this does not make for good long-term business relationships. The brief of most purchasing departments is to source supplies at the lowest possible price, and certainly in the public sector it is normal to go for the lowest tender, commensurate with delivery.

Suppliers, naturally, understand this mindset. However, put yourself in their shoes and things begin to look a bit different. It is in every organization's interests to have good relations with its suppliers, and this depends more than anything else on well-planned two-way communications, which can play a major role in improving business performance. Yet suppliers, as one of the stakeholder groups in a company, are often still treated in a less than friendly manner despite the company's dependency on their goodwill.

Owners and shareholders

Regardless of how well a business is doing, it has to keep its owners and shareholders properly informed about the current state of the organization. Owners invariably start many of the communication processes by asking endless questions of the board, to which they want answers.

Shareholders tend to be either institutional or private and, although both need to be kept informed, it is necessary to communicate effectively with brokers, analysts and the financial press as well, especially – but not necessarily only – in the case of larger companies.

'Ordinary' shareholders tend to be influenced by the financial press and larger companies often have a shareholder relationship manager whose sole job is to communicate with financial journalists, city analysts and major shareholders. The manager's role is to establish and keep communication channels open so that they will communicate their findings to a larger audience and hopefully in a manner which will be informed and fair rather than speculative.

The financial performance of a company, however, can only be one aspect of a company's communications agenda and therefore it cannot be isolated from the rest of the communications and PR functions of an organization. Financial PR needs to tie in with the messages being put out by the corporate affairs and PR departments, where these functions are split up – as is the case in many larger companies.

Corporate affairs

We all work in a world dominated by regulations that have been imposed by some governmental or professional body. We may not like it, but most of these regulations are the rule of law and every business needs to comply with them. Many impose considerable costs on a business and it makes sense, therefore, for organizations to monitor them and to try to influence the policymakers before their ideas become law.

Larger companies can employ lobbyists on their behalf both to monitor and to put forward their views to the bureaucrats. Smaller businesses can use their collective membership of bodies such as chambers of commerce or professional institutes to represent them.

Community relations

The perceptions of the people who live and work in the vicinity of your business can play an important role when you are attempting, for instance, to get planning permission for expansion or when trying to recruit the right local staff.

Many large organizations have programmes for establishing good community relations, which could, for example, include:

● sponsoring local cricket matches, concerts or art exhibitions
● maintaining the flower beds in the centres of traffic roundabouts
● taking disadvantaged kids for a weekend away.

At a time when all businesses are watching the pennies, a little bit of local largesse can go an extremely long way in helping get your local messages across.

Many larger firms actively encourage their employees' involvement in the community in some way. Some organizations second their staff to work in the locality on special community projects. Others actively support voluntary work or provide facilities for events. In doing so, companies make an effective bridge between themselves and the local community and improve the perception of themselves in the process.

Case study: PR and charitable activities

One of the major dairy products companies in the Middle East puts charitable functions at the very heart of the way it operates, with personal support often given by the CEO himself. The company regularly supports people with disabilities, special needs schools, the training of young people, and other charities too numerous to list here.

Of course, these charitable activities often lend themselves to useful photo opportunities with resultant media releases – something that this company has not been slow to pick up on. However, the essence of the scheme is at the core of its corporate ethos and it certainly doesn't do it any harm at all to be thought of as a thoroughly decent company.

These schemes work if they catch the public imagination. And they can be great fun too. The essence, though, is for the company to be seen to be putting something back into the community and being magnanimous about it.

Before embarking on a community relations programme, it is essential to...

- think through your parameters
- calculate how much time as well as money you want to devote to it
- appoint a member of staff as the main point of contact for all outside communications
- be realistic and try to choose a programme which has good photo opportunities.
- make sure you tell the world at large about it – locally, regionally and nationally, if not internationally.

Summary

Today we have seen that the ultimate objective of PR is to develop and build a sustainable corporate image and reputation for the business. This involves building a positive working environment with all those who can play a major role in improving the overall image of a firm among those with whom it deals. In the areas of quality and performance especially, expectations need to be communicated with all those involved in providing the service to the end client.

Although PR should have a separate and defined role of its own, it must also work in tandem with the marketing department if it is to have any hope of creating a favourable business climate for the company, as well as a reactive strategy to be able to deal efficiently with crisis situations.

Comprehensive PR strategies should educate, inform, explain and persuade. So knowing who it is you want to persuade or educate is an essential part of the PR mix. And once you know whom you want to talk to, the next thing to consider is the best ways of reaching them. And, as we will be finding out tomorrow, there are very many different communications channels available to reach your targets.

SUNDAY
MONDAY
TUESDAY
WEDNESDAY
THURSDAY
FRIDAY
SATURDAY

Fact-check (answers at the back)

1. When planning a PR strategy, which of these is the most important parameter to consider?
   a) What you want to say ❏
   b) To whom you wish to say it ❏
   c) Why you want to say it ❏
   d) All of the above ❏

2. When you go for a job interview, which of these is the most important aspect upon which you will be judged?
   a) How you dress ❏
   b) How you speak ❏
   c) What you say ❏
   d) Your mannerisms ❏

3. If you draw yourself a communications map...
   a) It is impossible to miss any of your target audiences ❏
   b) The relationships between your messages follow on from the relationships between target groups ❏
   c) The relationships between target groups follow on from the relationships between your messages ❏
   d) You need to highlight the different paths to reaching your target audiences ❏

4. Compared with 50 years ago...
   a) There is a greater need for companies to communicate with their customers ❏
   b) There is less of a need for companies to communicate with their customers ❏
   c) Increasing globalization means companies must always communicate with potential customers overseas ❏
   d) Customers now purchase more from a sense of need than they ever did before ❏

5. Which of these statements is false? PR can be used to help launch new products by...
   a) Differentiating them from other similar products ❏
   b) Placing advertisements strategically around a supermarket ❏
   c) Organizing special events ❏
   d) Distributing pamphlets and brochures ❏

6. The most common reason given by customers who desert a brand is that the company... ❏
   a) Offers poor service ❏
   b) Doesn't communicate with its customers ❏
   c) Is arrogant and doesn't listen to the needs of its customers ❏
   d) Prices its products too highly ❏

SUNDAY

MONDAY

TUESDAY

WEDNESDAY

THURSDAY

FRIDAY

SATURDAY

7. Most companies...
a) Know exactly what their customers want ❏
b) Have no idea what their customers really want ❏
c) Have a good idea what their customers want ❏
d) Use surveys to better understand how to sell their products to their customers ❏

8. Surveys are...
a) Useful for identifying trends in public perception ❏
b) Useful for accurately painting a picture of what a customer wants ❏
c) Not very useful since they take little account of people's perceptions ❏
d) A waste of time in some parts of the world because people say what is expected of them rather than what they actually feel ❏

9. Advertisers operate differently from PR practitioners since...
a) They need to worry more about the accuracy of what they say ❏
b) They tend to over-promote a product or service ❏
c) They can dictate what is and isn't said about their product ❏
d) They need to concentrate more on humour and approachability in getting their messages across. ❏

10. A company can always improve its relationship with its suppliers by...
a) Communicating better ❏
b) Insisting on the lowest possible price commensurate with delivery ❏
c) Comparing a supplier's costs with those of its competitors ❏
d) Seeing any problems from their point of view ❏

TUESDAY

Dealing with the media

It's a truism that one of the quickest and easiest routes to reach your target audiences is through journalists writing for magazines and newspapers, or broadcasting via TV or radio. For the past few years, there have also been the added major outlets provided by the Internet and social media – something we will be taking a look at tomorrow.

Good media relations can be critical for any business and play a significant role in the fortunes of a company. Handled correctly, your relationship with journalists can be advantageous for both sides – a win-win situation.

The secret is in striking a balance. Businesses should understand the importance of having good relationships with journalists. They can be a highly effective mouthpiece for communicating with your audiences, and it's in every company's interests to nurture a good relationship with them.

It's important to understand that a journalist has a job to do – that is, filling airtime if she's a broadcaster, or filling column inches if she's a print journalist. When you give a journalist a good story, you are actually doing her a favour. However, if she writes something about your organization that is correct but you don't like it, then, frankly, that's a fact of life and something you have to learn to live with.

Today, then, we will look at:

- the tricky balancing act a PR practitioner must perform working between company/client and the media
- building up relationships with journalists and reporters
- the importance of being aware of how the media – a newsroom, for example – works.

The PR as intermediary

The
company

The
media

It is the PR practitioner's role to act as intermediary between the people inside the organization and the journalists out in media-land. Almost all companies deal in the jargon of their trade, and it is up to the PR person to put all this into plain language that everyone can understand when presenting it to the outside world.

Identifying the right journalists to speak to for any story is as crucial as identifying your audiences in the first place. But journalists need good stories, so don't waste their time by giving them stories that are substandard or of not particular interest to them. They won't thank you for them and, worse still, you could badly damage your credibility with them in the future when you might most need them.

A reporter's need to talk to PR practitioners is dictated by events and circumstance. There are reporters who never need to deal with PR practitioners, although they may use a PR product, such as a press release. But reporters who avoid PR people shield themselves from potentially useful information resources, while PR practitioners who ignore the media limit their usefulness, and if they abuse editorial access they can even do the organization harm.

News media limitations

If you think about it, a newsroom is nothing more than an information factory. Raw material – the stories – come in at one end, they are refined and repackaged and are then sent out again. In most cases, news is time critical, but, apart from this, it is a straightforward process of repackaging stories to suit a particular audience.

Whether print or electronic, workers in this factory – the editors and reporters – process and publish content with an eye on consumer interest and/or accuracy and fairness to gain and keep readers, listeners or viewers. They define the news, and the order and presentation of stories. They essentially act as gatekeepers and filters of information at both fact gathering and editing levels, deciding at the end of the day what their readers and viewers will be told.

A typical newsroom is buried in information, but often this information might not be appropriate for the publication or broadcast station. Other information could be too costly to vet for accuracy so it will also end up in the waste bin.

Journalists in reality often have a difficult balancing act to play to satisfy their stakeholders:

- A reporter writing short stories for a business page from press releases and agency copy has a totally different job from that of an investigative reporter trying to prove that someone in authority has acted improperly.
- Everything in a news factory is geared to delivery of a product on time.
- One reporter might understand a complex explanation of a product or political situation better than another and accordingly treat the story in a totally different way.
- One reporter might be willing to spend extra time on a story or even report a story in which an editor has no interest.
- Some reporters are better visual, text and personal presenters than others.
- Reporters, too, are only human; and inevitably a reporter's beliefs about issues, persons and news can limit the type of stories he or she handles.

Getting messages out

If you wish your company news to be dissipated through traditional media outlets, it is essential to understand how and why the media operate in the way they do and the limitations to which any journalist has to work.

If your company's stories are not compelling, they will get lost in the information flow. It is also important to realize that if you get into the news, someone else doesn't. This competition for a reporter's attention creates a role for someone who knows the media and can deal effectively with them, such as you – the PR practitioner!

The corollary of this is that if your organization has compelling news, it may be published whether you like it or not. This is an even bigger reason to use practitioners who understand media operations and what can and cannot be expected to be achieved in mitigating negative news. Of course, if the news is positive, that same practitioner should best be able to advise on how to get maximum benefit from it.

Essentially, the PR expert should be gathering facts, setting up interviews, providing graphics and photos, gaining access for reporters to key people and assisting the reporter before and after news is published. This is a time-consuming process, but the results it can achieve make it well worthwhile.

The PR practitioner's role faces both ways – using knowledge of the news-gathering process to help his company tell a story and knowledge of his company to help the reporter relate the story to his target audiences. He is an intermediary who tries to satisfy both sides, although this is not always possible, and many is the time that PR people feel like piggy-in-the-middle, satisfying neither the media's appetite for facts nor their bosses' wish to protect themselves and their companies from criticism.

 PR men and women ultimately have loyalty to the organization that pays them and, as a result, they can be irritating barriers to reporters when they are not permitted to speak for the organization.

Reporters understand this dual role and appreciate knowledgeable practitioners who steer them in the right direction and save them time when reporting a story. However, a PR practitioner may want a reporter to focus on a story or facts the reporter considers irrelevant or ignore facts the journalist feels he or she needs. This, by its very nature, can create tension between the two.

If you, as a PR practitioner, want to gain the trust of a journalist, then it is beholden upon you to:

● deliver information and interviews the reporter needs
● provide clear and accurate facts to the reporter, whether good or bad
● be available when a reporter calls and handle his or her request quickly and accurately.

At the same time, you must always allow for the fact that ultimately your first priority must always be to your company rather than to the journalist.

Equally, a reporter gains credibility with a PR person by reporting fairly and accurately. If a PR person finds a reporter inaccurate, dilatory about interviews and elusive, the practitioner will go elsewhere to get a message out.

Dealing with reporters is like dealing with customers. You talk to some frequently and others only once. And, like customers, it is important for PR practitioners to treat reporters well. Most reporters are trustworthy professionals trying to do their jobs.

Because a reporter may deal with a PR practitioner only once or infrequently, it is up to you to know and become well known to reporters and not vice versa. Practitioners who avoid journalists or make no attempt to cultivate reporters consign themselves to low credibility with news media and lack of access when they need it.

However, it is no good thinking you can cultivate links with journalists by taking them out to dinner or even to an event such as horseracing if you are not able to talk meaningfully about your company. It may be very nice for the journalist to be taken out to dinner, but if she has nothing in the way of new information to show for her time spent, she will consider the whole exercise a waste of time.

It's not just about wining and dining!

This was the scenario faced day after day by PR executives in a certain defence company in the Middle East, which is probably best left incognito. They were given the unenviable instruction to cultivate relationships with local journalists, but at the same time they were not allowed to say anything whatsoever about the company, while the directors also had a policy of 'no comment' to any press enquiry. What did those directors sitting in their 'ivory towers', think they were hoping to achieve?

Limiting PR

In an era when some companies feel they have too much information written about them, they may limit their PR people to talking about issues that benefit the company only, such as marketing communications to boost awareness of products, services and brands. However, companies have more issues than marketing, and some reporters may want to explore them.

This is especially true with high-profile individuals and companies. When PR people become barriers to legitimate stories, they lose credibility with reporters who see individuals and companies as part of the larger environment and fair game for different kinds of stories. Reporters cannot be forced to focus only on a company's narrow, self-interested issues, and companies that subsume PR under marketing communications are, consciously or not, narrowing the issues a PR professional deals with and increasing their risks when issues arise that are out of the PR person's knowledge base.

Despite this, companies often place PR, or its equivalent, under a Chief Marketing Officer (CMO) whose focus is to build awareness and sales. This can work only if the CMO has as an expansive view of the company and its relationships to its stakeholders as the CEO. Unfortunately, that is rarely the case.

CEOs expect CMOs to build consumer loyalty, increase market share, and justify expenditures for marketing communications. CEOs want to know that money spent on marketing is actually resulting in profitable sales. The CMO, under pressure to show bottom-line results, is not going to spend much time on issues such as recruitment and retention, diversity, shareholder unhappiness, impacts of legislation, community pressure and a host of other stakeholder concerns that a typical PR department handles.

Thus, it is likely that a marketing communications focus will be forced to shift over time as other issues arise. The traditional structure is to have marketing-focused PR at the division or brand level and a corporate-focused department reporting directly to the CEO. This is generally regarded to be the best approach.

Truth, fact and perception

Reporters reach large numbers of individuals and directly influence opinions about reputations, products, services, issues or individuals. That's why they are so important,

and are worth cultivating. If reporters get it wrong, others suffer the consequences. But reporters are, after all, only human. Like all of us, they perceive the world from their own perspective. Ideally, we would all like to deal with reporters who have open minds, as we can then try to educate them to our point of view.

For example, a reporter who knows little about a particular market sector might not necessarily know what to ask a CEO about his or her business. The PR practitioner can help the reporter grasp details of that sector in order to conduct a meaningful interview. The practitioner will, of course, try to guide the reporter to relevant facts that place the company or client in the best light, and the reporter understands this. When a reporter knows a subject in depth, the PR practitioner can equally provide the supplementary facts that the journalist needs to write a story accurately.

Of course, PR practitioners may suggest to a reporter that one fact is more important than another, but the reporter may not judge it that way. As a result, fact ranking is inherently biased. However, that isn't necessarily harmful because reporters and editors tangle with fact and perception constantly. They are – or should be – masters in separating the two.

It is only when a reporter is manifestly wrong and out of control that a PR practitioner should even consider appealing to an editor over the reporter's head. This rarely happens because most journalists are taught to respect truth, fact and perception.

Changing opinion

What a journalist does with the facts he or she has gathered is also critical. Some news organizations believe a reporter's job is to state facts accurately and keep opinions to themselves. The BBC World Service radio station, for instance, keeps a clear dividing line between reporting facts in its news bulletins and commenting on those facts in its current affairs programming. BBC World News TV, on the other hand, regularly has comment mixed in with the straight reporting of news. Media get reputations based on how their reporters approach the issue of opinion and it is important for the PR person to understand this.

TIP *Practitioners should be informed about reporters they deal with and avoid situations where there is high risk. Learning about reporters comes from researching stories under their bylines and from experience with them.*

Of course, a journalist may have a hidden agenda, saying he is reporting such-and-such a story and then change course after an interview starts. Most journalists are trustworthy, but the PR practitioner should always be on their guard. With sensitive topics, it is essential to prepare the interviewee thoroughly for tough questions. This is why media training is important and why you should always insist that, at a minimum, your interviewee talks through the likely questions the journalist may throw at him. Clients who want to undertake interviews 'off the cuff' on tough topics are simply asking for trouble!

Trust is an essential component of PR–journalist interaction. If the PR practitioner is unknown to the reporter, there is no trust to begin with. If a PR practitioner says to a reporter 'I will get back to you', but never does, he or she will lose trust. If the PR practitioner is caught lying, or at least 'fabricating the truth', then trust could be lost for ever. If the practitioner faithfully returns calls, answers questions and plays straight with a reporter, a journalist will begin to trust him or her.

The same is true for journalists. An unknown journalist is trusted less than a known one. The journalist who 'will get back to you' but never does is not trusted and the journalist who burns sources by breaking his or her word to them loses them for ever. Truth, fact and perception live through interaction between reporters and PR practitioners.

Maintaining a spirit of accuracy is the best way to build credibility with reporters who value accuracy. Maintaining a spirit of service towards reporters and their needs enhances a practitioner's credibility because a reporter has to get a job done. Working with a deadline mentality supports reporters who live by deadlines.

Summary

Journalists can recognize a good story in seconds, so be sure to be able to tell yours simply and succinctly. Don't waste the journalist's time by rambling on about something he or she is unlikely to be interested in!

Understand who your audience is. Before you approach any media outlet, research it.

Build up relationships. By building relationships with reporters it means they are more likely to take your call when you've got an important story to tell; but treat everything as being 'on the record', no matter how close you are to the journalist.

Get your pitch right. Be upfront with the journalist about what you want. Wrap up your approach within 15 seconds and remember to ask if the journalist is on a deadline and if he or she would prefer you to call back later.

And remember: CEOs love coverage. A full-page story in a magazine or newspaper is something tangible you can show to your boss!

Fact-check (answers at the back)

1. PR practitioners need to keep up good relations with journalists so that...
   a) They aren't too nosey about your business ❏
   b) They can be an effective mouthpiece for your organization ❏
   c) They can be persuaded to retract pieces that are critical of your business ❏
   d) You can talk in confidence about your business without fear of being quoted ❏

2. When sending in some news to a journalist, which of these statements are not true?
   a) It is the journalist's job to write about it in a jargon-free way ❏
   b) It is the PR practitioner's job to explain it in jargon-free terms ❏
   c) Jargon has no place in news for general consumption ❏
   d) Jargon helps give a story more authority by setting the right tone ❏

3. Reporters only deal with PR people...
   a) When they want clarification on a news release they have received ❏
   b) In order to widen their information sources ❏
   c) When they want to speak to a CEO or other board member ❏
   d) When they are short of story ideas ❏

4. When journalists write up stories for their readers...
   a) It is up to the journalists themselves to decide what stories are suitable for their readership ❏
   b) A newspaper editor has final say over what goes into the paper ❏
   c) Journalists tend not to use stories that would cost them too much in time or resources to cover ❏
   d) The PR person should suggest story angles that a journalist can use ❏

5. When journalists write up stories from your press releases...
   a) It is incumbent upon them to contact you if there is something they do not understand ❏
   b) They will spend enough time on the story to get all the facts as they understand it ❏
   c) Their own beliefs and experience are likely to impact the way they cover the story ❏
   d) They are likely to hand over their material to another department if the subject matter is more suited to it ❏

6. When a journalist decides he or she wants to write something about your company, it is up to you, the PR practitioner, to...
a) Gather as much background information for the journalist as you can ❏
b) Provide graphics or photographs to accompany the story ❏
c) Give him or her access to key people and places which the journalist might not otherwise be able to find ❏
d) All of the above ❏

7. As a PR person...
a) You should always put the company's interests ahead of the journalist's ❏
b) You should always help the journalist get his/her story ❏
c) It is your responsibility to explain to the company management why it is necessary to help the journalist ❏
d) It is your responsibility to steer the journalist to cover the story in a certain way ❏

8. If a reporter misrepresents a company in his story, you as the PR practitioner should...
a) Demand a retraction at the next available opportunity ❏
b) Point out to the journalist the error of his or her ways and suggest a follow-up story to put the record straight ❏
c) Swallow your pride and put it down to experience ❏
d) Never deal with the reporter again ❏

9. If your boss is to be interviewed about a sensitive subject by a journalist...
a) She should always first have been media-trained ❏
b) She should rehearse answers to predictable questions in advance ❏
c) She should ask for a list of the questions before the interview ❏
d) She should simply decline to be interviewed if she is afraid of what the journalist might ask her ❏

10. When approaching a journalist with a story...
a) Always research the type of articles that journal covers before picking up the phone or sending the email ❏
b) Research when the next edition of the journal is going to press ❏
c) Never talk off the record when briefing the journalist ❏
d) All of the above ❏

WEDNESDAY

Social media

The world is changing, and with it a media revolution is taking place that is changing the 'normally accepted' ways of doing so many things.

According to media tycoon Rupert Murdoch, quoted in *Wired Magazine* way back in July 2006, 'to find something comparable, you have to go back 500 years to the printing press – the birth of mass media... Technology is shifting power away from editors, the publishers, the establishment, the media elite. Now it's the people who are taking control.'

Fifty years ago the 'media' consisted of newspapers and magazines, broadcast TV and radio and very little else. Now you can also add in cable TV, podcasts, social networks, satellite TV, the Internet, mobile Internet, text messaging, blogs and a whole lot else besides.

And in another 20 years? Who knows what?

One of the biggest challenges of this new order faced by PR professionals is the 'community' aspect of online communications. What is PR, after all, but the intention to communicate, build relationships and influence people? So new PR tools, media channels and a change of culture require nothing less than a completely new approach to this centuries-old art.

Today, then, we will see how:

- new media has revolutionized the business of PR and yet how fundamentally it has remained the same
- how to use blogging to develop your company's profile
- how to use social networking media such as Twitter and Facebook to generate interest and 'buzz' about your company and its products.

Plus ça change...

These are exciting times for PR professionals as what is happening now has never happened before. Online PR in particular is a completely new environment in which we need to relearn how to communicate – or our businesses will simply die. It is not an added extra, to be considered as a possibility when planning our PR strategies; it requires a completely new approach to our whole way of planning a PR campaign.

And yet... in some ways everything is exactly the same as ever it was – building relationships in order to influence. It could even be argued that online PR is actually a much purer form of what PR should have been and what it used to be before it got diverted and grew into so many other areas. Online PR actually puts things back where they should be. Online puts the 'public' back into 'public relations'!

Already, well over half of all online PR is no longer done by agencies. The PR 'leaders' of old are often way behind the mainstream players online. Digital PR offers huge new opportunities, but it is also seen by some old diehards as a threat. Depending on which PR magazine you read, it is claimed that around a half of all PR clients are dissatisfied with their agency's online PR offerings.

The biggest problem (or opportunity, depending on your point of view) is that the online world continues to change so fast. Probably the best way to get digital-savvy is to play around and get involved with the diff erent platforms.

 It is essential to integrate online PR with traditional forms of PR. One does not replace the other, but they must be used in partnership to get long-term overall success.

This new world order was aptly summed up by Sir Tim Berners-Lee – the 'father' of the Internet – who said:

'The idea of the Web as interaction between people is really what the Web is all about. That was what it was designed to be, as a collaborative space where people can interact.'

The numbers quoted by research agencies regarding Web statistics are truly awesome, and they seem to increase exponentially the moment a particular statistic is released. For instance:

● there were estimated to be in the region of 3 billion people online in 290 languages at the end of 2014 (source: www.internetworldstats.com)
● Google processes over 40,000 search queries every second or 1.2 trillion searches per year (source: www.internetlivestats.com)
● Wikipedia has over 4.9 million articles in English and is published online in 2902 languages (source: www.wikipedia.com)
● YouTube gets over 4 billion views per day (source: www.expandedramblings.com)
● Every second, around 6,000 tweets are tweeted on Twitter, which corresponds to around 200 billion tweets per year (source: www.expandedramblings.com)
● Facebook had over 600 million active users in the first quarter of 2015 (source: www.expandedramblings.com).

The effects of this were neatly summed up by Kathleen Schneider, an Executive Director of Dell Europe's marketing division when she told a conference that on any given day there were some 40,000 meaningful conversations about Dell products online. You can imagine the difficulty they must have in mapping these conversations!

Individuals have now got a disproportionate level of influence. A blogger in his or her bedroom can get a global readership – and this totally changes the perspective of the PR professional. On the positive side, there are a huge number of online forums, so this is a really good opportunity from a brand point of view for a company to listen to what people have to say about their brand or products.

Yet, despite the statistics, many company executives continue to act like King Canute and ignore this potential online opportunity. They still believe that a story appearing in print is worth much more to their business than a story appearing online. In part, this is a psychological reaction to placing more value on something physical – something you can actually hold in your hands. But consider this statement by Steve Fowler, Group Editor of *WhatCar?* magazine:

'I get 900,000+ visitors a week to whatcar.com and 127,000 readers a month to the magazine. But people still think that the magazine is much more valuable to be in.'

Consider, too, the statistics of readership of *The Guardian* newspaper. In July 2013, its print publication ran to approximately 189,000 copies. The newspaper's online edition was the third most widely read in the world as of June 2012, and its combined print and online editions reach nearly 9 million readers.

Add to this what Emily Bell, Editor of *Guardian Unlimited*, says – 'One-third of our traffic on *Guardian Unlimited* comes from stories more than a month old' – and you will see that the power of online coverage is not just in the sheer numbers of readers, but in the fact that your story stays in the public domain for a much longer time… in theory, for ever!

Now consider the following research about how journalists work, put together in a study by Middleberg/SNCR:

- 98% of journalists go online daily
  - 92% for article research
  - 81% to do searching
  - 76% to find new sources and experts
  - 73% to find press releases
- 56% of journalists also use blogs regularly
  - 33% to uncover breaking news or scandals.

What has become clear is that this revolution is not just about technology. It's a cultural shift. Advertising doesn't work as it once did and people are a lot more marketing-savvy than they used to be. Everything is becoming socialized. Consumers no longer accept being 'talked at' – they also want to 'talk with you'. All of this is good news for the PR profession because (in theory) this is what PR is all about!

 Simply put, some things just haven't changed: channels and media may change but the need for good PR remains constant.

Some things, though, have changed:

- It has never been cheaper or easier to produce content.
- Clients can bypass the media and communicate directly with their audiences.
- Audiences can easily communicate with each other on a large scale.
- The news cycle lasts longer – online news sources act like a permanent archive.

So it appears that PR models need to adapt to keep up with what is going on in the real world; and although it throws up new problems, the new technology can also help the overworked PR professional.

At the same time, as the numbers of influencers are both multiplying and changing, more effective messaging is required to reach this new body of people; and as the speed that messages spread through networks gets faster and faster, PR people need to adapt and develop their crisis procedures to handle much larger threats than ever before.

New opportunities

Although there are plenty of negatives that PR people need to adapt to with the new media era, there are also numerous new opportunities in online PR. For a start, you can now...

- **LISTEN** to your publics in ways which were previously not possible
- **IDENTIFY** influencers/issues related to your brand, organization and industry
- **ENGAGE** with multiple stakeholders in relevant and exciting ways
- **MEASURE** your outputs, and the resultant outcomes of your online efforts.

Interaction with media

The most obvious element of online PR is the way you can now interact with the media and the ease with which you can now find coverage of your organization. Remember that both negative as well as positive coverage has a much longer lifespan online than in traditional print.

News online is regularly refreshed, and because it is also searched for rather than simply viewed like a newspaper, it becomes much more relevant to the reader, who may even forward the article to a friend or colleague.

This means it is also now important for the PR professional to monitor online in order to keep up to speed with new developments in real time. The benefits cannot be overstated. At the very least, it acts as an early-warning system for potential crises. But it is also a global and highly cost-effective focus group that can give you excellent feedback on what the public really does think about your products and services.

With the advent of new media, too, there have appeared numerous niche publications that service a very precise (and often tightly focused) vertical market, giving you an excellent entrée to specific target groups that you might have found difficult to reach before. Normally, these are professionally managed sites that may even have a journalistic or editorial team, together with several contributors who are trade focused and could even be focused on location, interest topic or gender.

However, when informing new media about your company's news, the traditional elements of news releases (which we will be looking at in detail tomorrow) are as important as they ever were. All must contain a headline, core facts, possibly the inclusion of approved quotes, a 'Notes for Editors' section at the end and, of course, contact details. In addition, though, we now have the added benefits of being able to include navigation, hyperlinks in the body of the copy, links to previous coverage as well as links to other 'backgrounders' and FAQs (frequently asked questions).

Add to that an armoury of multimedia content, including video, audio and images, and your humble news release can take on a completely new and more exciting persona of its own.

Blogging

A recent newcomer to the Internet world of reporting has been the blogger – or 'web-logger' (a term originating in 1997, with the word 'blog' following two years later). Written in a conversational tone, blogs are now written by millions of people about many millions of subjects.

In some ways, blogs are just like conventional websites, except that... they are not! For a start, their content is frequently updated, they are written by the blogger him- or herself, and often contain multimedia. The blogosphere is a gender-neutral environment, with over half of bloggers in the 21–35 age group.

There are growing numbers of bloggers who post reviews on products and brands, and for the PR professional, therefore, blogs are not only important sources of information about a company's products and services, they are also a perfect platform for giving out information. Recently a number of websites have sprung up matching bloggers with large followings to companies wanting their products 'independently' written about. One might think that the ethics of this are questionable, but their popularity should not be underestimated.

In the 'blogosphere', they say there are three types of bloggers:

1 **thinkers** ...who create thoughts that weren't there before and who usually write long posts
2 **linkers** ...who act as filters for their readers so they return for more, and who tend to have short posts
3 **stinkers** ...who don't have much of an interest in what they're blogging about (they do it simply because it's fashionable) and who usually have very little to say.

The process for putting up a blog is not at all difficult, but it is not something that should be rushed into without any thought. Some companies start off with an internal blog that any staff member can contribute to. This is the ideal way to explore possibilities and to develop a corporate writing style.

You could get your new army of bloggers – together with other staff who are interested – to comment on the blogs, effectively expanding your site and developing your blogging culture.

Here are a few useful ground rules when establishing a company blogging site:

● When developing a corporate blogging policy, it is essential that your people understand what can and what cannot be posted. Obviously, due to the nature of a particular business, some things cannot be discussed, including commercially confidential information.
● You will need to remind employees that everything they write on the Web is in theory available for ever. Some companies tend to add a disclaimer to their blog sites stating that the bloggers' thoughts are not necessarily those of the company.
● When inviting comments from readers, it is a good idea to let people know that you retain the right to moderate any comments, and that you will not allow offensive comments to be published, but that you will not alter the contents of comments if they are included.

Don't be afraid to make some mistakes at the beginning. Everyone does, and it is an ideal way to learn. You will need to establish the strategy of your corporate blog and define an editorial policy. You want, after all, to engage with your readers, so you will need to create compelling content and post regularly to get them coming back for more. You will use keywords to ensure your blog is picked up by the search engines, and, of course, you will have a link to your blog from your company website's homepage.

Case study: Marriott Hotels

If you would like to see an excellent example of corporate blogging, then look no further than that of Marriott Hotels' Chairman and CEO, Bill Marriott (www.blogs. marriott.com). A self-styled 'Neanderthal' when it comes to blogging, Marriott posts on average a little more often than once a week. He doesn't use computers himself, but instead dictates to a member of his global communications team who goes away and transcribes his thoughts into a blog. She also reviews any comments received and then prints them out for him to read. If there are any he feels he wants to respond to, he tells her what he wants to say and she responds on his behalf.

On some occasions, fewer than ten people leave comments to his blog. However, on 20 September 2008 Bill Marriott posted about a bomb blast outside the Marriott hotel in Islamabad. He received 233 comments, overwhelming in their condolences and support. His three posts that week received 7,300 visits – about 200 per cent above its average weekly count.

This single occasion shows how useful the hotel company's blog turned out to be. It was an established blog that gave the company the means to reach out to customers and employees with an authentic expression of grief.

Marriott's Senior Director of Public Relations, John Wolf, said that the 'Senseless tragedy' post, together with the subsequent reaction, was a perfect example of everything they had hoped to accomplish when they first launched Bill Marriott's blog:

> *'The personal nature of Bill Marriott's blog has given the company much more than a face to a name. It has, as brand experts say, helped us make an 'emotional connection' with our customers and other constituents. And it has shaped what people think about us.'*

This was further reinforced by a comment from Marriott's Head of Communications, Kathleen Matthews:

> *'Marriott has made more than $5 million in bookings from people who clicked through to the reservation page from Marriott's blog.'*

 By encouraging comments to be posted (whether or not you choose first to moderate them), you can get instant feedback and measure the success of your blog.

There are plenty of free blog platforms you can use for your blogs. Perhaps the two most used are WordPress (www.wordpress.org) and Google's Blogger (www.blogger.com). Many are open source and allow you to fully customize the look and feel of the blog – which is important for branding purposes – as well as allowing you to add functional plugins.

Some bloggers can be very influential, especially in vertical markets. If you want to contact a blogger about his or her column, the rules of engagement are somewhat different from the way you might treat journalists, simply because the majority of bloggers are not journalists.

For a start, you should thoroughly read the blog before you make contact, and never send a press release unless you have prior approval. Many a company has found itself pilloried for trying to send press releases to bloggers.

Twitter

If social media is all about community, then Twitter is community gone wild. Many people miss the point of Twitter altogether, yet there must be something there if it now has over 302 million monthly active users

Many have criticized Twitter as encouraging an egocentric view of the world among the younger generation. On the other hand, it is Twitter that has been widely held to be the driving force for much of the social upheaval that has been seen across North Africa and the Middle East in recent times.

Today breaking news is often reported first by individuals on the scene who are equipped with nothing more than a mobile phone and a connection to a social media site, such as Twitter. For example, on 15 January 2009, when a US Airways aircraft went down into the Hudson River, it was a passenger on the first ferry to reach the stranded plane that disseminated the first photographs and reporting of the incident. This is also true of natural disasters and ongoing events such as the clashes in the Middle East.

Twitter appeals mostly to consumers who want to feel up to date and in the know, and as a means of gathering information about new products and services or other brand initiatives that would be of interest to them. It can also be used as a quasi-PR tool in its own right – as can be seen from the myriad of Tweets posted by entertainers and other celebrities who promote themselves and their movies using this micro-blogging site. We can now read the kind of news we earlier used to find in the tabloids, direct from the Twitter feeds of celebrities who are apparently ready to 'kiss and tell'.

Facebook

Of all the social media websites, Facebook has to be the outstanding success story. As of the first quarter of 2015, Facebook had 1.44 billion monthly active users, with an average time of 18 minutes spent per visit. It is the clear leader of the social networking pack, and according to figures from Mashable, if Facebook's user base continues to grow at its current rate, it could very soon surpass the number of people living in China – the world's most populous country (which ironically blocks Facebook along with other social media sites).

For this reason, it can certainly prove to be an inexpensive and highly effective tool in the PR armoury when used correctly. However, as ever, it is important to integrate it strategically with your overall PR plan.

The first issue to resolve is to identify your target audience. There is absolutely no point in getting hundreds of Facebook 'friends' who have no interest in your offerings. Facebook only permits a maximum of 5,000 'friends' so you need to create an efficient invitation strategy. Many companies nowadays add 'Like' icons to their web pages and marketing materials and it's surprising how many people click on them to show what they think of the product in question.

Here are a few useful pointers when seeking to exploit the Facebook phenomenon:

- You can use groups to find Facebookers with the same interests as your company's and those who belong in the same target audience. Monitor conversations closely to find out what's of interest to your audience, as well as any new group members who fit with your target audience.
- You can also use your Facebook friends' recommendations. Facebook recommends friends based on your current friends list and these recommendations are usually pretty accurate on relevance.
- Find out what is being said about your company and its products. You will need to do extensive research on the conversations taking place and the existing communities before taking part in them – this is time-consuming work.

- Once you have found them, you need to keep in touch with your new 'friends'. Make regular appropriate comments, and keep an eye on your friends' status updates, as great communication opportunities may be hidden there. Keep your profile up to date with accurate information and talk as if you are part of the group, not as a typical advertiser. Always link to your website and do not forget to put your contact information to encourage a dialogue.

Case study: Hennessy Cognac

By listening to mentions of its brand online, Hennessy Cognac discovered fans of their brand on a social networking site in the US for African Americans: BlackPlanet.com.

Analysis of these conversations, coupled with further marketing research, revealed their interests, preferences and how they interacted with the brand. Based on this data, Hennessy created a tour called Hennessy Artistry. They sponsored and set up partnerships with well-known African American musicians and held events and concerts in major cities across the US, always making content from these events available to post and share online.

Hennessy held a major celebrity-filled party in Chicago for their first new product in 50 years: Hennessy Black. Some 25 million people heard about this event through a number of different news websites and over 200 blogs and websites posted video interviews with some of the celebrities.

If you were to do a Google search now for Hennessy Black, you might be surprised at the number of blog entries, image entries and mentions of this one drink!

Listening to online conversations is a vital first step, allowing you to use the information garnered to allocate your resources wisely. You'll know where to start, whom to talk to, what content they respond to and what social sites you should be concentrating on. When you know the lie of the land, it's much easier to plot your roadmap.

Research and strategize

When considering your PR campaign using online tools, it is essential to establish clear objectives. You need to know what others are saying about you and your products. What news articles have been written about you? What have consumers and social media users said about you online? Where do these discussions take place? In blogs? forums? Twitter? Or everywhere?

Who are the people talking about you? Are they 'on your side'? Or are they castigating you for any reason? What does Google say about you? How do you feature in its search engine?

Now define your objectives. What are the stories you want to put across to online outlets? How are you going to build meaningful relationships with the online communities? What are the best platforms to reach them? Twitter? Blogs? YouTube? Facebook?

And how do you get your content to be visible in Google?

Summary

The fundamentals of online PR are in many ways just like regular PR. Some things will never change: a company is still judged on its products and services; its innovation; its workplace practices; its corporate governance; its leadership and its performance. We still operate with the intention to communicate, build relationships and exert influence. It is just that the toolbox has changed somewhat.

So what you need to do is:

- understand how your networked audiences work
- map your online environment to gain intelligence before planning your campaign
- be flexible with your tailored communications since no single approach is suitable for everybody
- be meaningful with your messages – avoid the spin, as you will be spotted a mile off
- be altruistic – because it will serve you in the long run
- be flexible so that you can react instantly to the feedback you receive
- never be afraid to experiment – the rules are still being written!

SUNDAY

MONDAY

TUESDAY

WEDNESDAY

THURSDAY

FRIDAY

SATURDAY

Fact-check (answers at the back)

1. Which of these statements is blatantly untrue?
   a) New media have raised the importance of journalists to a greater degree than ever before ❑
   b) Social media could eventually make professional journalism an obsolete profession because in the future ordinary people will report the facts ❑
   c) PR is losing out as the power of social networking grows exponentially ❑
   d) All of the above ❑

2. PR agencies need to catch up with Internet technologies...
   a) To seize new opportunities for their clients ❑
   b) To protect themselves from the threat of social networkers ❑
   c) To replace traditional ways of handling PR ❑
   d) To try to stop gossip and rumour ❑

3. When dealing with social networking over the Internet, PR professionals should...
   a) Try to get to know as many bloggers as possible in order to influence what they write ❑
   b) Send out press releases and other promotional material to as many bloggers as possible ❑
   c) Send out press releases and other promotional material to bloggers writing about the company's specific market sector ❑
   d) None of the above ❑

4. The number of online readers is higher than the number of readers of printed material; therefore...
   a) More PR value is to be gained by getting editorial in printed magazines ❑
   b) More PR value is to be gained by getting editorial in online forums than in magazines ❑
   c) Journalists place more weight on a story appearing in a printed journal than in an online site ❑
   d) Advertising online is more valuable than in printed journals ❑

5. Which of the following statements is not true?
   a) It is cheaper and easier to produce online content than printed material ❑
   b) Companies prefer to bypass the media and communicate directly with their customers ❑
   c) Customers can easily communicate with one another, bypassing the company in the process ❑
   d) In theory, online news lasts for ever ❑

6. PR people need to monitor mentions of a company online in order to...
   a) Get an early warning of possible problems with its products or brands ❑
   b) Find company mentions in printed media that they might have missed ❑
   c) Get feedback on its products or brands ❑
   d) All of the above ❑

7. Blogs are important sources of information for PR professionals because...
a) Many contain reviews on products and brands ❏
b) You can discover what is wrong with your customer care solutions ❏
c) You can find out what your competition is up to ❏
d) All of the above ❏

8. When posting up a company blog you should remember that...
a) Everything written is in theory available online for ever ❏
b) The bloggers' comments don't reflect the company's official line ❏
c) Offensive posts should be tempered down to make them more acceptable ❏
d) The inclusion of keywords allows your blog to be indexed by search engines ❏

9. Facebook is an ideal site for PR practitioners to use because...
a) It allows you to send out your company's details to as many as 5,000 people at a time ❏
b) It gives you the wherewithal to network with people who have common interests ❏
c) It gives you lists of people interested in your chosen market sector or interest group ❏
d) It is available in so many languages ❏

10. Twitter is a useful social networking platform because...
a) It is the preferred networking tool of the younger generation ❏
b) It is often first with up-to-date news ❏
c) Celebrities regularly use Twitter to 'kiss and tell' ❏
d) All of the above ❏

THURSDAY

Practical pointers for powerful press releases

Journalists the world over are sent a myriad of press releases every day. Some are well written, succinct and to the point. The majority, however, are not.

The unfortunate truth is that probably 99 per cent of press releases are thrown in the bin – and most of them are written by PR agencies! Journalists and editors take about five to ten seconds to decide whether or not to use a release. Those that are used and ultimately lead to a story tend to have certain qualities in common.

There are a number of reasons why so many releases fail to make the grade. Imagine that you are a busy journalist and you have a pile of releases sitting in the inbox of your email (for it's a fact that the majority of press releases these days are emailed to journalists rather than sent as hard copy, as was the norm until quite recently). The first one you read is florid in style, has typing errors and is laid out badly. The second one is short, to the point, and easy to read. Which would you prefer?

Today, then, we will learn about:

- what makes a release newsworthy – and specifically the 'five Ws'
- how to write a succinct and effective news release
- other kinds of PR product such as feature stories and media alerts
- how to enrich a release through pictures.

What is news?

Nowadays there is an enormous number of media categories to which you can target your news, including (but not limited to):

- the national press
- the regional press
- free newspapers ('freesheets')
- consumer magazines
- trade and technical publications
- broadcast media (radio/TV)
- the Internet.

Each sector has its own specific requirements, and the editorial material that you send out needs to be carefully targeted to match its specific needs. A story that is of interest to a local paper in Cardiff, for instance, will more than likely be binned if it is sent to a national newspaper or TV station.

One of the first things you as a PR practitioner needs to ask yourself is what actually constitutes news, since it can have so many different interpretations. In general, journalists tend to stick to a simple formula when considering whether a release will turn into a story. They ask themselves what are known colloquially as the 'five Ws' when reviewing your story:

- Who?
- What?
- Where?
- When?
- Why?

In addition, journalists will throw in an 'H' for good measure:

- How?

TIP *There's also one more question journalists will ask themselves, one that is regularly ignored by PR people desperate to get their clients into the media spotlight: Why should anyone care?*

If you want your story to make it into the news, it is important to hit all the right buttons with the media, in order to better your chances of seeing your story in the press.

What makes a story newsworthy?

Journalists have to find stories that are of interest to their audiences. They continually ask themselves what, if they were reading a publication or listening to a radio show, would jump out and appeal to them. So if you can put yourselves in the shoes of the journalist to whom you are targeting your release, once you can answer that question you've got the subject for your press release.

Typically, the following items regularly find their way into the media via news releases:

- new products
- improvements to products
- new contracts

- staff changes
- quarterly and annual figures
- achievements
- responses to a crisis
- special events
- charitable donations
- awards won
- promotions
- research findings
- human interest stories.

As producers of TV soap operas know only too well, disagreement or friction between two parties invariably leads to an interesting story. The simplest example is politics. Political arguments and posturing get a lot of press precisely because there is disagreement, conflict and unrest.

The unusual and unexpected also make interesting news, as do stories with universal appeal – such as the lifestyles of entertainers and celebrities. An appreciation of the components that go into what makes a story newsworthy will help you become successful in getting your key messages to your chosen audiences.

TIP *Before you do anything else, start with the 'Who cares?' test, and be strictly honest with yourself. Remember those 99 per cent of releases that end up in the bin. The media couldn't really care less about you or your business. What they are after is a good story.*

Journalists the world over are continually looking for good stories to fill their newspaper, magazine, radio or TV shows. All of them are under pressure from their editors to find stories that are of interest to their readers/listeners/viewers. So you can help them by meeting the aspirations of their audience. If you can show them how to do that, you're virtually guaranteed some coverage. Here are a few pointers:

- Different items, and the angle with which the stories are written, appeal to different segments of the press and public, so choose the media outlet (and the department within that outlet) carefully and make sure the release matches their needs.
- There is no such thing as a one-size-fits-all press release, and you have to be selective in what you send to whom. Are you sending a segment-specific story to general consumer media, for instance? If so, you are wasting your time (and, worse, the editors' time). As with most marketing, good news releases are a matter of being creative and thinking 'outside the box'.
- Find a special angle for your story. Does it have local appeal? Is there something unique about it? Can you combine two items such as a product announcement with a human-interest story to expand its appeal? You may have to write multiple specialized releases instead of one generic piece, but if you get more coverage, isn't it worth it?

What is the purpose of the release?

Many people the world over issue releases without a clear goal in mind, believing that it is important to appear in the media simply for the sake of being in the media. However, knowing what you are trying to achieve gives your writing focus and helps in the selection of distribution channels. It also means you have a far better way of tracking the overall effectiveness of your release.

Some of the most common reasons for sending out a release are:

- to increase or maintain awareness of your brand and products
- to establish credibility or authority within a particular market segment
- image building
- to become recognized as a source of expertise

- to help in the promotion of sales
- to drive traffic to a special event or to your website
- to change buyer/industry behaviour
- to expand your market share
- to comply with company regulations
- to increase the share price of your company.

How to write a press release

Start with a catchy, informative title. The **headline** is the most important part of your press release. It is the first thing the journalists see and if it doesn't grab their attention, they will read no further. It should be bold and interesting and, most importantly, it needs to stand out from all the other press releases with which it is in competition. If you read the headlines in your target publications, you will get a good feel for what works.

The reason that newspapers and magazines use bold, attention-grabbing headlines is that this is what draws in their readers. Exactly the same strategy should be used to grab the attention of the journalists you are trying to reach.

After the headline you should add a **dateline** at the beginning of your first paragraph. This comprises the city where your company or story is based – 'Glasgow' or 'Istanbul' – together with the date your release is being issued. This information is invaluable for journalists when they review the many releases they receive, as they may wish to 'park' your news until a later date, or to consign it to a particular section of their publication.

Next, you need to write **a solid, hard-hitting release** in a purely journalistic style (remember to answer the 'five Ws' the journalist will want to ask), keeping the language in the third person and completely free of hyperbole. Very importantly, make it perfectly clear *why* the reporter should cover your story.

The most important information should be at the top of your release, the next most important information in the second paragraph and so on down, so that if someone stops reading after the first or the second or the third paragraph, they still know what the entire story is about. (The person who reads further down only has more *detailed* information about the actual story being told.)

Refrain from verbosity, keeping out unnecessary adjectives and try to keep the release to one or two pages maximum whenever possible. If there is really a lot more information you have to tell journalists, consider adding a general invitation to contact you – 'For more information, contact ...'

Indeed, at the end of your release you should always give accurate **contact information**. Any journalist worth their salt is likely to need further information from you, if they are not simply going to copy-and-paste your release. So put a contact name, phone number(s) and email address.

Making your copy flow

One of the most common faults in news release writing is the use of sloppy language. This is particularly prevalent among those new to press release writing. Often they have picked up catchy phrases and are trying to emulate someone else's style. Perhaps they want to sound sophisticated or formal; are simply unsure of the key points they need to put across; may have padded out the release because they don't have enough information themselves, or they might not have critically read through their final offering.

And, dare one say it, in this social-media-centric new world, many aspiring PR hopefuls are quite simply illiterate!

 When you read through your copy, mentally eliminate words and phrases. If the piece reads well without that extra language, delete the surplus. It will make the final version easier to read and assimilate.

If you're writing about one of many products, concentrate solely on the product in question. It may be tempting to 'tell all' but, if it doesn't support the theme, resist the temptation. You can always put in extra information in a 'Notes for Editors' section at the end – but only if it really adds to the overall story.

Remember, too, that strong nouns and verbs work better than adjectives and adverbs. A few extra words in a sentence might not seem like much of a big deal, but when most of the sentences or paragraphs have 'a little extra', it slows the pace of your writing and buries your message. Don't make readers work to find out what you want to tell them! If you really need to add subjective information, such as opinions or grand claims, credit these to an executive in a quote, rather than stating them as fact – this adds to your credibility among those of a less trusting disposition.

News or feature?

The **news style** follows the conventional newspaper approach, summarizing, as we've already said, the story's 'who, what, why, when, where and how'.

A **feature story** press release, on the other hand, resembles a magazine article and is written in a more entertaining manner. The feature often sets the tone and background before introducing the main topic.

This type of release is sometimes more appropriate for specialist magazines that might have a small readership and hence a small budget; in which case, you could be doing the editor a favour by producing a ready-made package for him/her.

The regional press also has an increasing need for professionally written features which can be used with the minimum of reworking by their own journalists. Editors appreciate items which save time and money yet still offer a valuable contribution to their publication. Editorial budgets are under constant pressure, and free material is especially welcomed by the under-resourced free weekly regionals.

If your company people have expertise in a specific subject, encourage them to write an article targeted to the audience. Perhaps an editor would be interested in featuring a regular column from your company/client. Multiply that up, though, with the prevalence of online vertical market blogs and websites and suddenly it becomes a valuable piece of marketing that can project your organization into the limelight.

Feature articles, which are usually planned months in advance and are often focused on a particular event or time of year, should have a particular theme, either directly or indirectly connected with the company's services, and generally should avoid using the company name more than once or twice. Don't cram them full of promotional copy – it has to be of genuine *editorial* interest.

Another effective way of achieving coverage is to aim for inclusion in special feature supplements that your particular target media may run. Most publications publish feature lists well in advance, so it's worth obtaining copies of relevant lists at the beginning of the year to help you identify and plan material for the future, thus increasing the chances of achieving good coverage ahead of the competition. Your advertising department may already have this information to hand in order to plan its media buying.

The media alert

As well as straight news or feature releases, there is also a type of release called a **media alert**. Essentially, this is a memo from you to TV, radio and newspaper assignment editors, city desk editors and others who decide whether a particular news event is worth covering, to alert them about news conferences, charity events, publicity stunts and other events.

The point of the media alert is, in just a few seconds, to tell a journalist about the event, how to cover it and why it's important. Most publicists are pretty good on the first two points – almost all media alerts do a decent job of telling what the event is, where it will be held and what time it starts. It's the third aspect – the 'why' – that makes the real difference, though. And that's what you have to put most effort into.

Executive appointment release

Most businesses send out a brief release and headshot when someone new is hired or a major promotion is made. That may well get them into the 'People on the Move' column in the business section; but apart from being simply an ego trip for the employee, there's not an awful lot of merit to such a story.

Instead of announcing that someone has been hired or promoted, explain why the move is significant to the company – and perhaps the market – as a whole; and then offer someone for interview, too – assuming, that is, that they are media trained and comfortable giving interviews to the press.

A picture is worth a thousand words

If you're pitching stories about your company to the media, then including visual aids gives your release far greater impact. A good photo could even be enough to move your article from the back of a magazine to the front. Photos can be the deciding factor when you're pitching a story idea. An editor who knows that you can provide photos, or that their own photographer can take photos of something interesting, might be encouraged to say 'yes' to a story idea which might otherwise have found its way into the junk bin.

TIP *If a photographer from a newspaper or magazine does take photos at your company, you should never try to dictate or even 'suggest' what photo they should use with the article. The pictures are the property of the media outlet, which maintains full control over their use.*

Here are a few ground rules when providing and submitting photographical material:

- Put yourself in the position of the picture editor. What will his/her readers be interested in looking at? Certainly not pictures of two people signing a contract – these will go straight in the bin! So plan your pictures well in advance and write for your photographer a list of each shot you want to end up with, including details of the backgrounds and props required.
- Organize all the necessary props and backgrounds well in advance. Try to get the photographer to take a variety of shots so you have a range of different photos on the same subject for your photo library. This avoids having to send out the same old picture every time.
- Take care that the background will not merge with the subject when reproduced as a black-and-white picture. The colours may appear to be contrasting but could end up as one blur in a black-and-white photograph.
- Make sure that the picture you send can be easily cropped to fit all combinations of shapes on the page, such as landscape, portrait or square areas.
- With the ever-improving quality of digital photography and cheap scanners, many editors are only too happy to receive digital pictures, provided that the quality is good enough. Newspapers typically need a resolution not less than 200dpi (typically generated by a 3 or 4-megapixel camera), while magazines will require much better – 300dpi / 6 megapixel being the minimum acceptable quality. As most smartphones are capable of producing pictures at much better resolutions than this, and as output quality is getting even better and better, there is little excuse for not being able to send out a picture with your story nowadays.
- Provide a photo caption explaining the 'who, where, when, why and what' of the picture.
- Always submit photos with routine news announcements, if you want to have any hope of gaining coverage.
- In general, graphs and charts can tend to be a turn-off for ordinary consumer outlets, but speciality media, of course,

may well welcome pie charts, bar charts and other graphics if they can help their readers to understand complicated issues such as budgets. Sometimes, though, it is best to offer to supply information to media outlets so they can create their own graphics to accompany the article they're writing about.

Before sending out your release

Larger organizations invariably have a series of executives who have to review the release copy before it is sent out to the media. Ideally, the number of reviewers should not be too long (in order to maintain timeliness), and you should establish a process that indicates who has already reviewed the copy (such as dated initials).

If you're a small business owner, it is always a good idea to have someone else proofread your copy. Mistakes can easily slip in and it is very difficult to notice your own mistakes when you expect to see on the page something you meant to write.

Almost all publications have a hard-and-fast rule that all copy is checked by someone who did not write the item, specifically for this reason. Make sure you use this rule too!

Where should you distribute your release?

There are over 12,500 publications and newspapers and some 800 broadcast media in the UK alone; add in the many thousands of other media outlets around the world, you will realize that trying to establish which ones are relevant to you can be a somewhat laborious task.

Since an updated media contact list is essential, many companies send out their releases to a distribution service which takes on the responsibility of keeping such a list available for this purpose. Others purchase updated directories, which can be an expensive option if you do not send out that many releases. One of the easiest ways is to get on to the Internet and do a search of the media yourself, though this can be quite time-consuming.

While you're contacting conventional media outlets, don't forget to send information to Internet newsgroups, electronic newsletters and Web-based mailing lists that accept this type of news. Set up a newsroom on your own website so reporters can access your entire library of releases which you have sent out in the past. Apart from anything else, this makes their research work much easier for them.

This newsroom idea for your website can actually be used for a number of other purposes. For a start, why not prepare a brief biography of your company with a list of 'hot topics' the CEO or a manager could discuss? Journalists are always looking for new experts to interview, but invariably they go for the tried-and-trusted 'experts' for lack of time; so if you make it this easy for them, they will thank you!

Summary

Today we have seen that, to make any impact on journalists who, in the main, are inundated with news releases from all quarters, your release needs to answer the main six questions of 'who, what, where, why, when and how' within the first three paragraphs.

Your writing should be succinct – every word has to earn its place in your release. Ideally, you should make one major point in the opening sentence using not more than 25 words.

Keep paragraphs, particularly the first, to no more than about 40 words; and write in everyday speech, explaining anything the readers may not understand. Always be accurate when you quote someone, especially in headlines, and do not let your opinions get in the way of the story itself. The idea is to allow the readers to make up their minds from the facts as presented.

And, finally, if the story you send out could be libellous, send it to a lawyer first. The lawyer may be expensive, but could well cost less than the alternative!

Fact-check (answers at the back)

1. Many press releases get thrown away by journalists because...
   a) Most of them are written by PR agencies ❏
   b) They are un-newsworthy ❏
   c) They are full of typos and grammatical errors ❏
   d) Journalists have better access to stories than PR people ❏

2. Press releases can be used to publicize...
   a) New products ❏
   b) Human-interest stories ❏
   c) Special events ❏
   d) All of the above ❏

3. Which of the following statements is true?
   a) You need to make a journalist care about your business in order to even bother writing about it ❏
   b) You can help a journalist by giving him/her a story that will interest his/her readers ❏
   c) When sending out a press release, you should issue it to as many different sector-specific journalists as you can ❏
   d) Radio producers like to receive recorded press releases sent as mp3 files ❏

4. The main reason for sending out a release is...
   a) To appear in as many media outlets as possible ❏
   b) To gauge public opinion of what your company is up to ❏
   c) To increase or maintain awareness of your brand and products ❏
   d) To comply with company regulations ❏

5. When thinking about the contents of your release, the most important part is...
   a) The 'Notes for Editors' section at the end ❏
   b) The contact number which a journalist can use to get in touch with you ❏
   c) The headline ❏
   d) The first paragraph ❏

6. When writing a release, which of the following is true?
   a) You should remove all adjectives and adverbs to make the text flow better ❏
   b) If your release is a little on the long side you should make the typeface slightly smaller to fit it all into two pages ❏
   c) You should always include an email address and phone number for further information ❏
   d) You should type it in Times New Roman font, with double spacing and ragged left aligned right ❏

7. When deciding what goes into a release, which of the following is true?
   a) Modifier words add excitement to your overall writing style ❏
   b) Opinions should be put in quotes and attributed to someone in authority ❏
   c) Adding quotes gives credibility to your story ❏
   d) The present tense is often better at generating attention than using the past tense ❏

8. Feature press releases are often sent to journalists because...

a) They can be written in a more entertaining manner by the PR officer ❑

b) They can save the media outlet time and money ❑

c) They have more credibility coming from a company in that sector ❑

d) They are cheaper than paying for 'advertorials' ❑

9. Media alerts are useful for telling journalists...

a) About a new service or product your company is issuing ❑

b) Why they should cover a particular event ❑

c) That you will be attending a national exhibition ❑

d) About your annual profit forecast ❑

10. When considering sending out an executive appointment release, you should...

a) List all recent senior management promotions ❑

b) Offer up the appointee for interview ❑

c) Attach a head-and-shoulders picture of the appointee ❑

d) Explain why the appointment is significant for the company ❑

FRIDAY

Marketing communications

Business success depends on your customers, and since the advent of the Internet and other technologies, never have real customer communications been more important.

'Enlightened' companies of yesteryear were good at basic customer care solutions such as training their receptionists to be polite and helpful, but most customers today never set eyes on the receptionist, let alone talk on the phone to anyone there. In this new Internet world, today's organization needs to concentrate on marketing communications as well as providing customer service and aftercare in a way that will retain those customers in the long term.

Marketing communications cover many different areas, from deciding who prospective customers are in the first place – as well as their needs and desires – to letting them know what products are available. The PR professional plays a crucial part in this communications effort.

Today, then, we will be looking at the two main platforms that a PR professional uses in communicating messages:

- the company website newsroom
- events, from trade exhibitions to conferences and seminars.

Measuring opinion

As is common with many PR activities, measuring opinion is a crucial part of building an appropriate and successful communications plan. A company that gets genuine feedback from its customers and target groups will be better equipped to know how to impart its own messages that it wants to get across. As we saw on Thursday, the advent of the Internet has made the process of surveying customers and prospects much easier and cheaper than it ever was.

Such surveys can be used for identifying trends and for getting a 'broad-brush' picture in order to identify areas for more in-depth and specific research, which can then be undertaken in a more specialized and focused way. The trouble is, however, that these surveys tend to deal in generalities.

Promoting your goods and services can include a wide variety of activities for gaining the attention of your prospects, and these can say a lot about your company and its products. In the main, they are – or should be – all about tempting your prospects by creating a feeling of excitement.

However, it's a sad fact that in today's technologically driven world, the PR community is doing pretty badly when it comes to putting together a useful online media resource.

Because so many journalists say that the information found on a corporate website has an impact on their decision to include that company in a story, having the right information on your website can make an enormous difference to whether you are getting media coverage. Companies and organizations which provide the right information can maximize their relationships with journalists, resulting in better coverage and increased efficiency of resources.

So just what kind of information do journalists want? Typically, the top three items your website newsroom should provide are:

1 **press releases** – including both current and archived releases (make sure you have an easy search option!)
2 **24-hour contact information** – including a specific contact person by name, title and phone number and how to reach them

3 **corporate information** – including a company profile, statistics and executive biographies.

The last should comprise information that will help journalists gain an insight into the company and its management. You should think about including some basic facts and figures: number of employees, annual sales, and any information that places your company in context.

Events as part of a PR communication strategy

Every business gets involved with events in one way or another, whether it is a major corporate exhibition or something staged at a local hall to promote a local product or interest group, and usually it is the PR department which will be charged with putting it on and making it a success.

Events come in all shapes and sizes, from trade exhibitions to focused seminars and conferences, but they all need clear objectives if they are to be measured a success.

You don't necessarily need a large budget to stage a successful event, but nothing can substitute for meticulous planning with a good team of people, and you will benefit from someone who has a great deal of lateral vision when planning for contingencies.

It is a sad fact of life that very many people set off in a forlorn attempt at organizing something without either having thought through thoroughly what it is they actually hope to achieve, or allowing enough time to do it.

It is also a truism that company management very often do not appreciate the time and effort needed to organize a successful event, while it is almost routine to find exhibitors who leave everything to the last minute and then expect everyone else to drop whatever they are doing simply to rescue them from the mess of their own making.

A successful organizer should be able to think laterally and pull together a disparate series of events, while being able to think things through logically, quickly and clearly, especially at times of great pressure. If he or she can keep a sense of perspective and a sense of humour, that is all for the better!

The type of event

So, having got over the initial euphoria of being asked to stage an event, the first thing you have to do is sit down for a moment and define what it is you are actually hoping to achieve. Only once you have done that can you even hope to make the correct decisions as to the type of event that will be most appropriate. Ask yourself:

● Is the objective to impart information, or to act as an incentive?
● Will you be launching or raising the profile of a product, handing out awards, reinforcing relationships with customers, exhorting others to do better, or something else?
● Who will be your audience? Will it be held purely within the confines of your organization, or will it be open to the world at large?

Under the headline of 'Events' you can also include the likes of gala dinners, award ceremonies and activity days – such as golf, motor racing, horse racing and general team building. Whatever it is, it needs to be planned in the same manner as conferences and exhibitions, and suitable checklists need to be created so that nothing is forgotten.

In business, it is often necessary to attempt to change the way people think and how they regard your company. That, of course, is one of the most basic remits of PR. A well-planned and executed conference can enthuse a sales force, persuade employees to change their working practices or launch a new or unfamiliar product to a specialist audience. Above all, it can enable people to come together and communicate with one another more effectively.

Choosing the best venue

Having decided upon the type of event you wish to put on, one of the most important decisions that any events organizer has to make is the choice of venue, for this one factor can literally make or break the smooth running and success of any 'do', be it a conference, exhibition or seminar. Unfortunately, many venues that market themselves for events are in reality quite unsuitable. First impressions count, and if you are let down by the location, inadequate local services or poor service from the event location itself, then your event can quite literally be ruined.

Start by drawing up a list of those all-important questions:

● How long will the event be?
● How many delegates are likely to be attending?
● How far will they have to travel?
● What budget is allowed?
● Will anyone need overnight accommodation?

Having decided the price band, check out the travel times and suitability of various locations. It simply is no good selecting a superb location if it is difficult to find or access is poor. Of course, it is absolutely essential for the organizer to pay a visit to each possible venue, preferably incognito and also when another meeting is going on. That way you are much more likely to be able to weigh up the look and feel of the place and judge its suitability. Inspections are important because you can never tell from a brochure or website what the downsides could be.

You should always check out the following:

- the attitude of the staff
- the quality of accommodation
- the condition of the furnishings
- the formality of the venue or room
- the ease of moving from one area to another – such as from the room or hall to the coffee area
- the adequacy of the room's ventilation
- the availability of small meeting rooms if delegates need to be split up into small groups
- the rules regarding the positioning of banners and posters
- whether the venue will be shared with other organizations
- the provision of telephones.

Make sure you speak to the person responsible for handling corporate events; don't be satisfied with just speaking to the sales manager. You need to know exactly what you can expect to get, and you should not hold back on any questions for fear of offending anyone.

Preparation and rehearsal

In preparing for an event, some kind of time planner is invaluable in order to graphically interpret timelines and dependencies. Many organizers make use of computer software such as Microsoft's Project, which prepares Gantt charts and dependencies.

It cannot be overstressed how important it is to plan for all eventualities – as far as you are able. Without adequate planning, the opportunities for confusion, oversight and mistakes are considerable.

Rehearsals, of course, are an absolute necessity. Don't allow anyone involved with the show to skip the main rehearsals, especially the final rehearsal – and that includes everyone right up to the Chief Executive!

Check that the lighting is adequate for the speaker to be able to read his/her notes and that the lectern is the right height for him/her. Time each element of the show, in case adjustments need to be made while the event is actually taking place.

Remember, too, that by taking part in a public event you are (probably) opening up your company to public scrutiny. If the stand or venue looks shoddy, then what does that say about your organization? If staff members are ill informed or rude, then what confidence will your potential customers have in the company in general? On the other hand, if the stand is smart, and your staff are polite, approachable and knowledgeable, then the image of your company will be positive for all to see and remember.

Letting people know

Ultimately, though, it doesn't matter how good an event you have arranged – if no one knows about it, you are wasting your time. Yet regularly exhibitors and conference organizers fail in this most basic task of letting anyone know they are taking part in an exhibition, or staging a must-attend conference.

We have already seen that there a number of ways of letting people know about an event – not least through the use of news releases and media alerts (see Thursday). Your promotional activities should concentrate on attracting visitors to your event. You might choose to attract as many as possible or identify your most likely prospects in advance and do everything in your promotional power to attract them to your show. Neither method is right or wrong; rather, it depends on the reasons for holding the event in the first place.

Pre-show promotion should generate more visitors than you would normally have got, had you just sat back and hoped for the best. It should also generate press coverage, which may influence some to pay you a visit; others who cannot attend for whatever reason will still have been introduced to your products and services.

As we have already seen, journalists need good stories. You, on the other hand, need publicity. So what better than making sure you create a win-win situation by following these tips to maximize your press coverage:

- Write one press release for each product or service you wish to promote.
- If you are launching a new product or service, make sure this is clearly highlighted at the top of your release.
- Give relevant figures to back up your story, especially product prices and the value of new contracts. This gives the resulting story more colour and depth and it saves journalists having to ferret out the information themselves.
- Include colour photographs if they help the story along.
- Send in your story in plenty of time. It is simply no good sending something in two days before the event and hoping that it will get space. Journalists plan well in advance, and so should you!
- If you are taking space at someone else's event, then find out if they have a press office or PR representative and, if they do, then keep them fully informed of any product launches or other news you might have. You might even find there is an official show preview that is mailed to potential visitors to raise their interest. If you can get a story about your company into one of these publications, then the chances are that you will get more interest during the actual event itself.
- At all times you should concentrate on selling the benefits of your product or service, not just its features. It is said that most people buy primarily to assuage their feelings of fear or greed. If a customer is considering buying a product or service, she is not necessarily interested in the physical attributes of the product, but in what benefits will accrue to her if she does make the purchase.

It is all too easy for someone who is close to a product or story to gloss over information that is crucial to someone else's appreciation of it. One excellent exercise is to add the phrase 'which means that' in order to link a feature with the benefits it brings. You could even end your publicity with a one-liner such as 'Following this event, delegates will be able to…' and list a few positive key factors to which the delegate can relate.

Dealing with the media

If you want to maximize the coverage of your event in the media, then you will want to follow a few simple rules:

- As we have already seen, seek coverage only for newsworthy events.
- Distribute a clear, concise media advisory.
- Make the event easily accessible to the media.
- Have a professional, friendly media check-in.
- Provide a useful press kit.
- Give journalists their own clear space at the event.
- In order to increase the likelihood that the media will cover your press conference you could send out both a 'media advisory', followed a few days later by a press release.

If you expect live television coverage of your event, bear in mind that parking can be tricky for microwave or satellite trucks, whose crews need to run cables to the camera platform and send a signal back to their station. Consult the venue manager to find out where television stations have parked their trucks in the past. In order to encourage and prepare for television coverage, include on your media advisory the phrase, 'Please advise if you are planning live coverage.'

Have a table specifically for media people to check in so that your PR staff know exactly who attended. Offer journalists a press kit and a copy of any other materials you want them to have, then escort them to a designated media area where they can work comfortably during the event. Nowadays it is normal for reporters to have their own laptop computers, so ensure there are enough power sockets for them. Snacks and drinks are also well appreciated, though not obligatory.

All the while, try to offer optimum conditions to reporters since this will increase the chances of media coverage for your event, while enabling the reporters to focus on your key messages rather than be distracted by the difficulties of covering it.

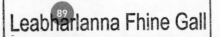

Leabharlanna Fhine Gall

If things go wrong...

Live events are the classic time for 'Murphy's Law' to rear its ugly head: if anything can go wrong, now is the time that it will happen.

TIP *Think through your worst-case scenarios. Perhaps your guest speaker fails to show up, the lights fuse, the set falls apart or the air conditioning breaks down.*

Of course, it is impossible to plan for every possible disaster scenario, but worrying unduly is not the same as making plans for what you would do should things go wrong. Every event organizer needs the ability to think ahead, quickly troubleshoot any problem and come up with a fix. It may not be an elegant fix, but if it gets you out of a hole, then no one is going to complain. It is at times like these that you will be very glad you timed every element of the event during rehearsals.

The way in which you react to a crisis is also very important. Think of yourself as the proverbial duck – serenely gliding through the water, while paddling furiously underneath the surface. If you remain cool, calm and collected, you will have a pacifying effect on everyone else. If others see you as being totally in control it will improve the chances of the event not turning into a disaster.

Summary

Inevitably, PR professionals need to concentrate a great deal not only on showing off the company in a good light, but also on helping to promote its products and services.

You can promote your goods and services in a number of ways to gain the attention of your prospects by creating a feeling of excitement.

Normally, it will be the PR department which is the main body looking after a corporate website. Very many journalists use the information on corporate websites, so it is important that they are kept up to date with the latest news and information. Companies that provide this information can maximize their relationships with journalists, resulting in better coverage.

Most PR departments, too, get involved with – or even plan – corporate events, be they exhibitions, seminars, conferences or other types of show. For all of these it is essential to plan thoroughly, leaving nothing to chance.

You can measure the success of an event in many ways, but by focusing on the objectives throughout your planning stages, you can ensure the basic foundations from which a successful event can be achieved.

SUNDAY
MONDAY
TUESDAY
WEDNESDAY
THURSDAY
FRIDAY
SATURDAY

Fact-check (answers at the back)

1. Corporate websites which contain a 'newsroom' for media to access should include...
   a) Press releases – both current and archived ❑
   b) 24-hour contact information ❑
   c) A company profile ❑
   d) All of the above ❑

2. The most important thing you need to decide before staging any event is...
   a) Where you will stage it ❑
   b) How much budget you have ❑
   c) What you want to achieve ❑
   d) Whom you will invite ❑

3. The most important consideration when choosing a location for an event is...
   a) What it looks like ❑
   b) How far it is from your company headquarters ❑
   c) How well it looks after its guests ❑
   d) How good a menu it can offer ❑

4. When going to check out a venue for a conference, you should get all the relevant facts directly from...
   a) The sales manager ❑
   b) The receptionist ❑
   c) The head chef ❑
   d) The corporate events organizer ❑

5. When rehearsing a conference, which of the following are essential prerequisites?
   a) Timing the CEO's speech ❑
   b) Checking lighting and sound equipment ❑
   c) Keeping anyone out who has no need to be there ❑
   d) All of the above ❑

6. A good sign that your pre-show publicity has worked is...
   a) You get more visitors to your show than you would normally have expected ❑
   b) Your show gets front-page billing on the show daily newspaper ❑
   c) Your CEO is pleased with the turnout for his/her speech ❑
   d) None of the above ❑

7. When sending out information about your participation at a major conference, you should...
   a) Send it out three months ahead of the event to give journalists plenty of time to plan their coverage of your company ❑
   b) Send it out one month ahead of the event together with a couple of photographs of your CEO ❑
   c) Send it out one week ahead of the event together with an invitation to visit your stand ❑
   d) Send out a series of releases, spaced one week apart, and incorporate ongoing stories and photographs to keep the journalists' interest up ❑

8. When putting together a release about your new product, you should...
a) Concentrate on selling the benefits it offers users ❏
b) Concentrate on highlighting its features ❏
c) Appeal to customers' greed and fears ❏
d) None of the above ❏

9. When media attend one of your events, your most important consideration is...
a) Having a specific area for reporters to check in ❏
b) Offering your invited media a press kit about the event ❏
c) Providing them with tea or coffee ❏
d) Providing a designated working area with power sockets and Internet access ❏

10. If things go badly wrong at an event you have organized, you should...
a) Learn a valuable lesson ❏
b) Try to think laterally and come up with a solution ❏
c) Remain cool, calm and collected ❏
d) All of the above ❏

SATURDAY

Internal PR

For a number of years, downsizing of companies has been a worldwide phenomenon, as technology obviates the need to have the large workforces that were so necessary in the past.

When structures were split horizontally between departments and vertically between the various layers of management, many people were stopped from communicating outside their own specific departments. They were not able to see the overall picture of what the company was trying to achieve. In addition, many of the people who make up a company have little or no contact with the company's customers and are therefore limited in what they can contribute to improve the business.

The struggle for competitive edge, however, now means that the staff are much more important than they ever used to be, for without their empathy, flexibility, creativity and intuitive thinking, there is little to differentiate one business from another. For this reason, the need for internal communications has never been more important to a company's prospects.

Today, then, we will look at:

- how effective internal PR is vital for the wellbeing of the staff as well as the company more generally
- using employee surveys to launch successful two-way communication within a company
- the different conduits for staff communication.

A neglected audience

We have already seen that any communication process starts with the identification of the publics to be addressed, together with an analysis of what key messages need to be got across to them. Every organization has a large number of target audiences, all different from one another, and a clear understanding of fixed objectives is essential in the identification of the various publics involved.

However, in every organization there is always one target audience that is both close to the company while also often neglected: the employees. This is most often shown up when a message reaches the staff via the outside world, rather than being directly delivered to them in the first instance.

There are a number of reasons why organizations need to be concerned about internal communications. Not least is the fact that there is a legal requirement across much of Europe for organizations to communicate with their workforce. Legal requirements aside, however, organizations that put employee communications on the back burner are simply asking for trouble, especially in this age of mass communications and social networking.

It is far too simplistic to think that staff are merely interested in their salary, career progression, improvement of professional skills and the availability of information. There are plenty of other less obvious, sometimes intangible, interests, not least the sense of being part of a team, the role and participation in the development of the business and so on.

Given these elements, both material and non-material, it can be seen that employee satisfaction is an important objective for any organization and needs to be properly addressed, not least through a comprehensive communications programme. It could even be argued that the effort expended on employee communications should be at least of equal importance to the amount of effort exerted on external relations.

As such, internal relations are very much a part of the communications mix and therefore part of the basic responsibilities of a PR practitioner, who should be highly conscious that the quality of internal relations is a critical element of each organizational system. Indeed, one could go further by saying the quality of internal relations directly influences all external relations in terms of effectiveness of the relationship itself, while enabling a company to accomplish its goals in the most effective ways, in less time and with lower costs.

 TIP *The PR practitioner's role nowadays seems more and more intricately woven in with that of the human resources (HR) department, concentrating on the delivery of company messages to the workforce.*

The science of internal or employee communications is probably bound more by the principles of psychology than any other PR discipline, since it is essential to tap into people's innermost feelings and use them in a positive way to help the communication process across the company. That means understanding that immediate reactions to problems often disguise deeper feelings, which need to be unlocked.

Delivering the goods depends on a director's ability to harness the ideas and creativity of his/her staff, who need to be fired up and encouraged to behave in a way that supports the long-term ambitions of the organization. Employees all have needs and aspirations that need to be met if the directors and senior management want to get the best out of them. Good communications up and down the workforce are therefore an essential part of the management of a company.

Involving the workforce

In principle, the best way to communicate with the workforce is to make the bulk of general information available to everybody in the organization, with exclusions being as few as possible. This is where the communications department and HR need to work in close harmony for effective internal exchanges to take place.

Employees need to feel that they, too, can help set the agenda, allowing them to bring up problems that they face or anticipate and encouraging them to be discussed openly. Problems, especially, faced by those at the sharp end of the business need to be addressed quickly if customers are not to become aware of internal trouble within the organization.

The reality in many companies does not make comfortable reading. Some of the best news stories an organization has to tell about itself are well-known to everyone except its employees. This can happen for many reasons, but invariably the organization can become so focused on getting its message out to the world at large that management just assumes everyone working for the company already knows what is going on, as if by a process of osmosis; or they simply fail to dedicate the time and energy to keep their own people in the loop. This can invariably lead to poor morale, increased turnover of staff, and a bad image problem for the company.

Yet it is one of the greatest truisms of all time that a company's best ambassadors tend to be those self-same staff whom management are routinely ignoring in their day-to-day working lives. Since most people assume that anyone who works for a salary is only in it for the money, someone who sings the praises of their employer's products has a very high level of credibility to any audience, be they friends, relatives or complete strangers.

TIP *Motivating your employees to speak out positively on behalf of their employer could not be easier. Simply tell them what the company is doing, what their role is, why it is important, and solicit their comments and suggestions. This internal communication is an essential element of PR.*

In internal communications, more than in any other PR discipline, honesty is definitely the best policy. People will often accept bad news if they are well informed and given the reasons why something has happened. But if you are caught hiding some of the key facts, you lose credibility, and it will be very hard to regain the employees' trust after that.

Surprisingly, many HR departments communicate too little and they're only too happy to hand everything over to the PR or communications department. HR people tend to regard themselves as the technicians handling pay schemes, leave entitlement and such like, whereas PR people are seen as the spin doctors whose main function is to put the message across, however unpalatable it might be.

But getting staff on side with the company they work for is one of the easiest aspects of the PR function. You could, for instance:

- conduct monthly or quarterly meetings where all employees are given an update on the organization's goals and progress
- hold regular meetings offering recognition to staff for their contributions
- solicit suggestions for improvements in the workplace
- give employees a first look at new products or services and the plans to promote them

- produce a monthly employee newsletter and/or create an intranet site that discusses company news and highlights employee initiatives; better still set up a closed user group on a social media site – WeChat is an excellent option, for instance – so that everyone is connected and feels part of the corporate family
- select a charitable cause that is related to the company's mission and provides employees with an incentive to volunteer, and then publicize their efforts.

One of the key principles of effective internal communication is not just to tell your people what is going on, but also to explain why something is happening in the way it is. If your people don't understand the problem that you are attempting to solve, they won't feel any ownership of the solution you are proposing, and as a result not be proactive in its implementation. When employees are informed about what their organization is doing and recognized for their role in its success, they will become some of your best ambassadors.

In order to develop a strategy of actively encouraging two-way employee communication, senior management need to create an environment in which this type of interaction will thrive. This invariably means ensuring that there is commitment to full internal communications all the way through the organization and that all employees are empowered to an appropriate degree in implementing company policy.

The employee survey

An employee survey is an excellent way of gauging where to start this process while at the same time signalling to the workforce that their opinion is actually wanted and will be listened to. Nowadays it can easily be carried out using an intranet with answers emailed to a central processing department, or even using one of the many external survey websites that promise to keep your employees' answers confidential. You could, of course, still use paper-based forms, though this takes up more time and resources and offers little in the way of benefits over easily set-up online surveys.

Anonymity is essential in the employee survey, and everyone must be convinced that what they say won't be held against them in the future. For this reason, many companies prefer to use outside survey firms that can guarantee anonymity and impartiality.

Remember, though, that if you invite comment and criticism you will be expected to address the real issues which can no longer be simply swept under the carpet. Only undertake a survey if there is real commitment from the highest levels of the company. And just because a company has gone to the lengths of having a written policy of employee empowerment and of full internal communication, it will be a total waste of time if those at the top of the hierarchical tree don't live by that policy themselves. It simply is not good enough to have a 'don't do as I do – do as I say' policy, for all respect and support from your employees will disappear in an instant.

First, in order to gather some demographic information – to put the data into some kind of meaningful sequence – you need to ask your staff to complete some basic questions, such as their level within the organization, their location, length of service and age – for it is a well-known fact that such basics can play an important part in the way people feel about a company.

CAN I ASK YOU A FEW QUESTIONS?

Next, you should ask them to indicate on a scale of one to five their level of agreement to a number of statements you make – for example:

- I enjoy working for this company.
- I understand the company's goals and priorities.
- The company has a good reputation.
- I am confident in the future of the company.
- Senior management does a good job of managing the company overall.
- My function is well managed.
- I feel loyal to the company.

Surveys completed online can have their data sorted and databased very quickly and easily with the plethora of online tools available (many of them free), and can give an instant snapshot of the mood of the company. Importantly, this data also gives a good indication of where you can now concentrate your efforts for further research.

 As well as producing a great deal of useful information, a survey can have a very positive effect on staff morale.

Don't forget to give feedback on the analysis of the results – ensuring, of course, that confidentiality is maintained, or your next survey will not yield much of any use.

Strategizing your internal communications

A communications strategy needs to encompass many things, if it is to be successful. For a start, it needs to reflect a company-wide culture in which values are of more importance than mere words written in the company mission statement (which in practice few employees ever bother reading, let alone remembering!). Most importantly, messages across the company need to be consistent if they are to be trusted and people are to understand and play their full role in any changes that will affect both themselves and the company.

So in putting together your communications plan, you need to make it sufficiently detailed to define what methods and conduits are to be used throughout the organization, while ensuring that it is the strategy that defines the media, rather than the media dictating what strategy is to be implemented. This often means that there will be no substitute on occasion for real face-to-face communications between management and staff.

In all communities – be they companies, schools, or any other type of gathering – there is invariably an informal communications network in place, regardless of what management sets out to do. It's called the gossip network and it's fed by rumour. An internal communications strategy therefore needs to be able to work with this or counteract it effectively, and the best method of doing this is to ensure that staff are empowered to give feedback and positive suggestions and that their feedback is actually acted upon in some way.

Questions and comments from the workforce should be actively encouraged and, wherever possible, this information should be freely disseminated so that employee trust is built up over a period of time.

Sometimes it may be necessary for totally different messages to be given out to internal staff than to external audiences – such as when a company is going through difficult times when it needs its own people to understand what is going on, but which, for obvious reasons, it doesn't want leaked to the outside world. However, in normal circumstances steps need to be taken to ensure that internal messages don't conflict with external messages in order to risk credibility with either audience.

Naturally, there are times when confidentiality demands that delicate information cannot be released early. However, in that case employees should always be told at the same time as an official announcement. Lack of information is the number-one breeding ground for rumour, and once started it is very difficult to counteract. Staff will want the facts, and want them straight.

This is one of the main reasons why internal communications are best driven by the PR department as a whole, rather than delegating it to others such as HR, who of course will still need to have a major input to the plan.

During times of crisis, the support of staff becomes especially valuable, as their friends and relatives seek their account of events, and as talented and motivated participants consider whether or not to remain with the organization. With the prospect of reputational crises having the power to destroy brand value and even bring a company to its knees, it can be quite revealing to see how internal communications is suddenly given a boost in value by senior managers following a period of crisis.

Organizations that have a mature internal communications plan in place often have contingency plans prepared, too. They are more likely to have a well-rehearsed line management communications plan that can be swung into action at the slightest sign of any trouble brewing on the horizon. Less mature employee communications departments may find it difficult to bring the attention of senior managers to bear on their internal audience, especially when critical stakeholders such as investors or customers appear to be a more pressing problem.

In essence, the real benefits of employee communications come from getting the listening right, rather than telling people what's going on as viewed from the perspective of top management. It's the front-line staff after all who are usually closest to any customer problems, and by listening to what they have to say you will have a better-motivated workforce.

Feedback from all your people – but especially those at the sharp end – is essential and a non-confrontational feedback system will always give the company information it can use to improve matters.

Conduits for your messages

Formal channels of internal communications typically fall into one of four broad categories:

1 **electronic** – delivered and/or accessed by smartphone, computer, telephone, television or other devices
2 **print** – such as magazines, newsletters, brochures, posters, and communication packs

3 **face to face** – one-on-one and one-to-many forums where people physically talk to one another, such as team meetings or briefings, conferences and round-table discussions
4 **workspace environment** – including noticeboards and TV screens.

In general terms, 'face-to-face' communications are always the most appropriate where there is a risk of misunderstandings occurring or when emotions are running high.

Informal channels can often turn out to be more effective than official channels, and will often stimulate and create discussion and dialogue between groups. For this reason, if for no other, a company should actually encourage its people to chat at the water-cooler or coffee machine, over the social network, and so on. What used to be considered a time-waster has now been re-evaluated by many leading companies and is actually an excellent way of passing on crucial messages and stimulating ideas within a company.

Long gone are the days of so-called 'line manager cascade' when information was sent down the line to local supervisors, who were expected to deliver it to their subordinates without any corruption, interpretation or deviation. If the company had the foresight, these line managers would also be encouraged to report feedback up the line to the top management. But what a circuitous process! How could anyone have ever expected such a laborious process to generate anything really useful?

Thankfully, in more recent years the received wisdom has changed and now concentrates on empowering managers to facilitate discussion rather than simply cascading those management messages to the boredom of all concerned.

Promoting internal communications

As with all PR activities, there are numerous channels you can now use to get your chosen messages to your employees. Many companies, for instance, have an intranet system of some sort which should be kept up to date with how the business is getting on, key contracts won, major exhibitions and the like attended, and perhaps even a regular blog from one of the board members.

Each department could also have its own page on this site updating employees on local progress, and how what they are doing ties in with the aspirations of the company as a whole. You could even devolve this system down to project level, if appropriate. Companies such as China Central Television in Beijing, use the social app WeChat (Weixin) for their information cascading. Even individual programmes routinely set up WeChat groups and everyone involved instantly knows what is going on.

Here are some other ideas for facilitating internal communications:

- As well as, or instead of, an intranet, the main company website is a very important outlet for updating your people, for the majority of staff will visit it from time to time. As well as a weekly or monthly ezine that can be directed at both external and internal audiences, some kind of organizational calendar can give visibility to outside events with which the company is in some way involved.
- The use of email is also extremely important in delivering information to staff, be it in the form of activity reports or direct messages. Aim to communicate something, at the very least, on a weekly basis to your staff.
- Company newsletters can also be delivered as hard copy, rather than as ezines, especially in manufacturing companies where many of the workforce might not have access to a computer for all or parts of the day. But as the world becomes ever more social-media focused, such traditional forms of communication are fast disappearing.
- And, of course, staff meetings, team meetings, coffee meetings, huddles in the coffee area and so on should all be actively encouraged to improve the feeling in all of your employees that they belong to an exclusive club – your company!

Summary

The principles of good internal communication can be encapsulated in that well-worn phrase: 'Do unto others as you would have them do unto you.' In other words, consider how you would like to receive messages rather than how you would impart them; think how you might react to someone else giving you the particular message you want to give out yourself; and then impart your message in the way you know will be received in the best possible way.

For a highly effective internal communications strategy and plan:

- employee-focused communications must be led from the top
- employee communications are not optional extras – they are an essential part of business
- there must be integration between internal and external communications
- communication is a two-way process
- senior managers must always practise what they preach
- consistency of message is vital
- timing of the message is crucial.

SUNDAY
MONDAY
TUESDAY
WEDNESDAY
THURSDAY
FRIDAY
SATURDAY

Fact-check (answers at the back)

1. Companies should always communicate with their staff...
   a) Because it is a legal requirement in Europe ❏
   (b) Because staff like to feel part of a team ❏
   c) To address employee satisfaction ❏
   d) To encourage their staff to feel motivated for the company ❏

2. Staff should be encouraged to bring up problems that they face, in order to:
   a) Improve customer expectations ❏
   b) Help the overall efforts of the company ❏
   c) Help set the agenda of the company ❏
   d) Prevent them bottling up their feelings ❏

3. Not keeping staff informed about company business can...
   a) Lead to poor morale ❏
   b) Encourage staff to leave the business in search of pastures new ❏
   c) Create a bad public image for the company ❏
   d) All of the above ❏

4. When communicating with staff, the most important thing they want to know is...
   a) What is going on across the company ❏
   b) Why the company is doing what it is doing ❏
   c) That what they are doing has an important role to play in the overall aims of the company ❏
   d) Where they sit in the overall remuneration schemes of the company ❏

5. When undertaking an employee survey, the most important thing to consider is...
   a) Keeping all answers anonymous and confidential ❏
   b) How easily the data from the answers can be collected ❏
   c) How to inform the employees what the survey results reveal ❏
   d) Not making promises that the company cannot keep ❏

6. When surveying your staff, you should always ask them...
   a) Where they work ❏
   b) How old they are ❏
   c) Whether they understand the company's overall goals ❏
   d) All of the above ❏

7. All internal communications need to be made...
a) In close collaboration with the HR department ❑
b) Consistently across the entire workforce ❑
c) Dependent on what communications conduits are available ❑
d) On a face-to-face basis between management and staff ❑

8. An informal gossip network should be encouraged by...
a) Spreading rumours about the company ❑
b) Providing coffee machines where people can congregate ❑
c) Making it easy for employees to give feedback to management ❑
d) Letting employees know about confidential decisions in the boardroom ❑

9. The main value of employee communication comes from...
a) Listening to staff ❑
b) Letting staff know what is going on at senior management level ❑
c) Telling staff what is expected of them ❑
d) Being able to use staff at times of crisis ❑

10. The best conduit for staff communication...
a) Is through the use of newsletters and noticeboards ❑
b) Via email and ezines ❑
c) Face to face ❑
d) Depends on circumstances ❑

7 × 7

1 Seven things to ponder over

- If you don't want to take risks, the PR industry isn't for you.
  If you take no risks, you will accomplish nothing.
- The PR industry changes each and every day. Become the change you want to see.
- Arrogance can be a problem in the PR industry. Too much, and you'll never learn what you need for tomorrow.
- Don't take yourself too seriously. A sense of humour is essential to success.
- Reading and consuming information is absolutely essential. If you're not constantly consuming information that will make you smarter, you might as well just give up.
- The quality of your work is all you have. Your reputation is based on it.
- There is nothing to replace good, old-fashioned experience – something that the under-30s could do well to remember.

2 Seven ways to improve your press releases

- Optimizing your press release for search engines to find it does not mean cramming so many keywords in that it becomes unreadable. Concentrate on the message, rather than how many times you can mention your company's name.

- Press releases are not advertisements, so make sure they don't read like one. Get rid of all hyperbole and stick to the facts.
- Less is more. Concentrate on quality, not quantity. It is usually more difficult to say what you want to say in fewer words than by being verbose; but the end result is always better.
- Get to the point. The journalist should be able to find out what the press release is about by reading just the first paragraph. He can then decide if he wants to read more or not. The most important information (who, what, when, where and how) is placed at the top, followed by the minor details.
- Avoid jargon in all your PRLs. Your release should be comprehensible to everyone, not just those who work in your industry.
- Find a solid news angle that focuses on some unique function of your business. Then, craft your headline around that news angle. Always ask that most basic of questions: why should anyone care?
- Proofread your release, then proofread it again. Better still ask someone else to proofread your PRL. Without proofreading, you risk sending out a press release that's riddled with typos and grammatical errors, which doesn't exactly command respect from editors or online readers.

3 Seven says to get your internal messages across

- Be clear and concise. Using technical jargon can lead to confusion and misunderstanding.
- Set the tone at the top. Senior management needs to be visible and accessible, and they must understand the correlation between strategic employee communication and the achievement of organizational goals.
- Most people need to hear or see a message multiple times, in multiple ways, to understand it completely. Distribute your messages electronically, in writing, face to face, and in meetings.
- When you prioritize your communications, your employees should hear it from you before they hear it from anyone else; they shouldn't be surprised by a media report.
- If you say you will address a situation in a certain way, do it. If you don't, you're undermining your credibility.
- Nothing beats human interaction. Most employees want to hear news and information from their supervisors. Managers need to be trained in how to communicate, and they need to have the right tools at hand.
- One-way communication is a thing of the past. Individuals should be empowered to talk back; and feeling 'listened to' enhances their feelings of trust.

4 Seven social media sites you can't do without

- We all know that Facebook is the top social networking site bar none. If you're not on Facebook, your online strategy hasn't even begun.
- Like Facebook, Twitter has also changed dramatically and is now a top source for real-time news sharing.
- Making its debut in 2011, Google+ is the fastest growing social network the web has ever seen. And with the power of Google behind it, it can only go from strength to strength.
- Where does everyone go to watch video content online? After Google, YouTube is the second largest search engine. The perfect place to park company videos, product videos and even speeches – as long as they are good and actually say something!
- Anyone who needs to make professional connections should be on LinkedIn. Individuals can promote themselves and their businesses, outline their education and work experience, make connections with other professionals, interact in group discussions, post job ads or apply for jobs.
- Instagram has grown to be one of the most popular social networks for photo sharing that the mobile web has ever seen. It's the ultimate social network for sharing real-time photos and short videos while on the go. Use it for real-time communications from your company.

- Tumblr is an extremely popular social blogging platform heavily used by teens and younger users. As such if your company targets the younger age ranges, this app should definitely be on your list.

5 Seven things to think about for your company website's newsroom

- If you're not archiving press releases on your company's website, you could be missing out on valuable press coverage. Reporters increasingly rely on the Internet to conduct research on the issues and industries they cover.
- Include background information on your company, short bios of top managers, product details, an image gallery, contact names, event details with press kits, email addresses and phone numbers for reporters to make follow-up calls.
- Where appropriate, use hyperlinks within the text to help reporters access any further information on a particular topic. Potential clients will also appreciate this background information, so don't set up special log-ins for the media.
- For contact information, NEVER make this section into a form. Offer direct contact information so journalists can reach your media contact s directly.
- Label information clearly. Separate information under clear labels such as News Releases, Articles, White papers, Podcasts. Don't lump information together. Also, if you have various types of visitors, create different sections such as 'For Journalists' and 'For Investors'.

- Add a search feature. Some visitors may want to find information quickly through search. Make sure a search function is available that catalogues not only your written materials, but your images, videos and podcasts too. Search engines such as Google make adding this facility a doddle.
- Share your content. Use an AddTag to allow visitors to easily share your news through RSS feeds, Digg, MySpace, Facebook, and so on.

6 Seven things a typical PR specialist might have to do in a day

- Prepare press releases and contact people in the media who might print or broadcast their company's material.
- Arrange appointments and conduct programmes to maintain contact between organization representatives and their target audiences.
- Represent the company at community projects.
- Prepare film, slide, or other visual presentations for meetings.
- Plan conventions and other events.
- Prepare annual reports and write proposals for various projects.
- Monitor social media for mentions of the company or organization.

7 Seven great PR quotes

- 'Since we cannot change reality, let us change the eyes which see reality.' Nikos Kazantzakis

- 'PR means telling the truth and working ethically – even when all the media want is headlines and all the public wants is scapegoats. Public relations fails when there is no integrity.' Viv Segal
- 'It takes 20 years to build a reputation and five minutes to ruin it. If you think about that, you'll do things differently.' Warren Buffet
- 'What kills a skunk is the publicity it gives itself.' Abraham Lincoln
- 'If I was down to the last dollar of my marketing budget I'd spend it on PR!' Bill Gates
- 'Publicity is absolutely critical. A good PR story is infinitely more effective than a front page ad.' Richard Branson
- 'All the president is, is a glorified public relations man who spends his time flattering, kissing, and kicking people to get them to do what they are supposed to do anyway.' Harry S. Truman

Answers

Sunday: 1a; 2d; 3d; 4c; 5b; 6d; 7c; 8c; 9b; 10c

Monday: 1d; 2c; 3c; 4d; 5c; 6c; 7c; 8b; 9d; 10c

Tuesday: 1c; 2d; 3d; 4c; 5c; 6a; 7d; 8c; 9c; 10c

Wednesday: 1a; 2a; 3c; 4b; 5b; 6d; 7d; 8c; 9d; 10b

Thursday: 1d; 2d; 3c; 4b; 5c; 6c; 7a; 8b; 9a; 10d

Friday: 1c; 2d; 3c; 4d; 5d; 6b; 7d; 8c; 9d; 10d

Saturday: 1d; 2c; 3d; 4a; 5d; 6c; 7b; 8c; 9d; 10b

Notes

ALSO AVAILABLE IN THE 'IN A WEEK' SERIES

MORE TITLES AVAILABLE IN THE 'IN A WEEK' SERIES

ADVANCED NEGOTIATION SKILLS • ASSERTIVENESS • BUSINESS ECONOMICS • COACHING • COPYWRITING • DECISION MAKING • DIFFICULT CONVERSATIONS • ECOMMERCE • FINANCE FOR NON-FINANCIAL MANAGERS • JOB INTERVIEWS • MANAGING STRESS AT WORK • MANAGING YOUR BOSS • MANAGING YOURSELF • MINDFULNESS AT WORK • NEGOTIATION SKILLS • NLP • PEOPLE SKILLS • PSYCHOMETRIC TESTING • SEO AND SEARCH MARKETING • SOCIAL MEDIA MARKETING • START YOUR OWN BUSINESS • STRATEGY • SUCCESSFUL SELLING • UNDERSTANDING AND INTERPRETING ACCOUNTS

For information about other titles in the 'In A Week' series, please visit www.teachyourself.co.uk

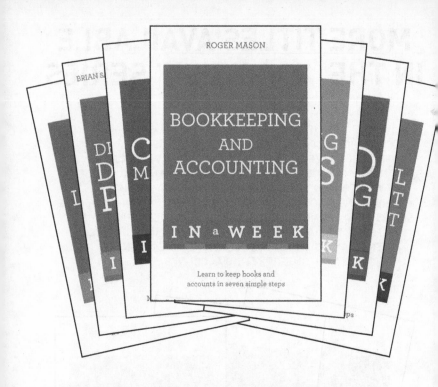